WEIGHT
WATCHERS®
1993

PERSONAL
DAILY
PLANNER

NAL BOOKS

WEIGHT WATCHERS is a registered trademark
of Weight Watchers International, Inc.

NAL BOOKS
Published by the Penguin Group
Penguin Books USA Inc., 375 Hudson Street,
New York, New York 10014, U.S.A.
Penguin Books Ltd, 27 Wrights Lane,
London W8 5TZ, England
Penguin Books Australia Ltd, Ringwood,
Victoria, Australia
Penguin Books Canada Ltd, 10 Alcorn Avenue,
Toronto, Ontario, Canada M4V 3B2
Penguin Books (N.Z.) Ltd, 182–190 Wairau Road,
Auckland 10, New Zealand

Penguin Books Ltd, Registered Offices:
Harmondsworth, Middlesex, England

Published by NAL Books, an imprint of New American
Library, a division of Penguin Books USA Inc.

First Printing, August, 1992
10 9 8 7 6 5 4 3 2 1

 REGISTERED TRADEMARK—MARCA REGISTRADA

Printed in the United States of America
Set in Garamond Light and Helvetica

Designed by Steven N. Stathakis

Congratulations! You're about to take charge of your life and your weight. In this handy personal planner, you can record your daily food intake, log your exercise time, be inspired by real-life motivational tips, and keep track of your important appointments. And you can start using it today!

In addition, there are twenty-six brand new, easy-to-fix recipes to add variety to your meals. With your health in mind, we've noted those recipes which are reduced in cholesterol, fat, and sodium.

Here is just what you need: easy, delicious family suppers like Fisherman's Pie, Veal Stew with Dumplings, and Savory Chicken Loaf. For your lunch on the go, try Pizza Muffins or a Peanut Butter–Banana Sandwich. And when you're in the mood for a snack, plan to have a Strawberry Meringue Tart with Chocolate Syrup.

Carry this planner with you every day; it fits easily into your pocket or purse for easy reference. The specially commissioned painting on the cover will not only please your eye but will also serve as a gentle reminder of the emphasis you will be placing on carbohydrates, vegetables, and fruits in your menu planning.

Here's a special tip to get you started: record all your meals and snacks each day. Then, when you've had a particularly successful week, refer back to your food choices for that week to help you plan future meals. At the end of this year, when your book is filled with the record of your successful weight-loss journey, you can look back with pride on your accomplishments and ahead to future goals, made possible by your new, strong self-image, self-confidence, and skills you have acquired for a healthy and rewarding lifestyle.

SEPTEMBER 1992

SUNDAY	MONDAY	TUESDAY	WEDNESDAY
		1	2
6	7 LABOR DAY	8	9
13	14	15	16
20	21	22	23
27	28 FIRST DAY OF ROSH HASHANAH	29	30

SEPTEMBER 1992

THURSDAY	FRIDAY	SATURDAY	NOTES
3	4	5	
10	11	12	
17	18	19	
24	25	26	

W E E K L Y   F O O D   D I A R Y

	MONDAY	TUESDAY	WEDNESDAY	THURSDAY	FRIDAY	SATURDAY	SUNDAY
DAILY TOTALS	MILK FAT PROTEIN VEG BREAD FRUIT	MILK FAT PROTEIN VEG BREAD FRUIT	MILK FAT PROTEIN VEG BREAD FRUIT	MILK FAT PROTEIN VEG BREAD FRUIT	MILK FAT PROTEIN VEG BREAD FRUIT	MILK FAT PROTEIN VEG BREAD FRUIT	MILK FAT PROTEIN VEG BREAD FRUIT
BREAKFAST							
LUNCH							
DINNER							
SNACKS							

FLOATER®

OPTIONAL CALORIES

WEEKLY LIMITS EGGS/ORGAN MEAT _____ CHEESE/MEAT _____

I will attend my Weight Watchers meeting this week on _____

AUGUST / SEPTEMBER 1992

WEIGHT WATCHERS

GOAL:

MONDAY 31

TUESDAY 1

WEDNESDAY 2

THURSDAY 3

FRIDAY 4

SATURDAY 5 / SUNDAY 6

Changing from a "diet mentality" to a lifestyle approach to weight loss includes changing all negative, self-defeating thoughts into positive ones. One way to do this is to think about your goal each day. Imagine how you'll feel and look when you've succeeded!

WEEKLY FOOD DIARY

	MONDAY	TUESDAY	WEDNESDAY	THURSDAY	FRIDAY	SATURDAY	SUNDAY
TOTAL DAILYS	MILK ___ FAT ___ PROTEIN ___ VEG ___ BREAD ___ FRUIT ___	MILK ___ FAT ___ PROTEIN ___ VEG ___ BREAD ___ FRUIT ___	MILK ___ FAT ___ PROTEIN ___ VEG ___ BREAD ___ FRUIT ___	MILK ___ FAT ___ PROTEIN ___ VEG ___ BREAD ___ FRUIT ___	MILK ___ FAT ___ PROTEIN ___ VEG ___ BREAD ___ FRUIT ___	MILK ___ FAT ___ PROTEIN ___ VEG ___ BREAD ___ FRUIT ___	MILK ___ FAT ___ PROTEIN ___ VEG ___ BREAD ___ FRUIT ___
BREAKFAST							
LUNCH							
DINNER							
SNACKS							

WEEKLY LIMITS EGGS/ORGAN MEAT _____ CHEESE/MEAT _____ FLOATER® _____

OPTIONAL CALORIES _____

I will attend my Weight Watchers meeting this week on _____

SEPTEMBER 1992

GOAL :

MONDAY 7 / LABOR DAY

TUESDAY 8

WEDNESDAY 9

THURSDAY 10

FRIDAY 11

SATURDAY 12 / SUNDAY 13

Before you overeat on impulse or because of stress, pause for a minute. Take a deep breath. Think about the meal or snack you are about to eat. Make sure the food is one that fits within your weight-loss program, is something you really want, and is a food you're going to enjoy.

WEEKLY FOOD DIARY

	MONDAY	TUESDAY	WEDNESDAY	THURSDAY	FRIDAY	SATURDAY	SUNDAY
DAILY TOTALS	MILK FAT PROTEIN VEG BREAD FRUIT	MILK FAT PROTEIN VEG BREAD FRUIT	MILK FAT PROTEIN VEG BREAD FRUIT	MILK FAT PROTEIN VEG BREAD FRUIT	MILK FAT PROTEIN VEG BREAD FRUIT	MILK FAT PROTEIN VEG BREAD FRUIT	MILK FAT PROTEIN VEG BREAD FRUIT
BREAKFAST							
LUNCH							
DINNER							
SNACKS							

WEEKLY LIMITS EGGS/ORGAN MEAT ———— CHEESE/MEAT ————

I will attend my Weight Watchers meeting this week on ————

FLOATER®

OPTIONAL CALORIES

SEPTEMBER 1992

GOAL:

MONDAY 14

TUESDAY 15

WEDNESDAY 16

THURSDAY 17

FRIDAY 18

SATURDAY 19 / SUNDAY 20

If possible, don't eat alone. Don't read while you eat; it only makes you eat faster.

It's OK to lose the weight slowly; too fast and too soon tempts you to revert and regain.

—*Patricia F. Colosimo*

WEEKLY FOOD DIARY

	MONDAY	TUESDAY	WEDNESDAY	THURSDAY	FRIDAY	SATURDAY	SUNDAY
DAILY TOTALS	MILK FAT PROTEIN VEG BREAD FRUIT	MILK FAT PROTEIN VEG BREAD FRUIT	MILK FAT PROTEIN VEG BREAD FRUIT	MILK FAT PROTEIN VEG BREAD FRUIT	MILK FAT PROTEIN VEG BREAD FRUIT	MILK FAT PROTEIN VEG BREAD FRUIT	MILK FAT PROTEIN VEG BREAD FRUIT
BREAKFAST							
LUNCH							
DINNER							
SNACKS							

WEEKLY LIMITS EGGS/ORGAN MEAT _____ CHEESE/MEAT _____ FLOATER™ _____

OPTIONAL CALORIES _____

I will attend my Weight Watchers meeting this week on _____

SEPTEMBER 1992

GOAL:

MONDAY 21

TUESDAY 22

WEDNESDAY 23

THURSDAY 24

FRIDAY 25

SATURDAY 26 / SUNDAY 27

Relax before you eat; don't eat to relax.

OCTOBER 1992

SUNDAY	MONDAY	TUESDAY	WEDNESDAY
4	5	6	7 YOM KIPPUR
11	12 COLUMBUS DAY	13	14
18	19	20	21
25 DST ENDS	26	27	28

OCTOBER 1992

THURSDAY	FRIDAY	SATURDAY	NOTES
1	2	3	
8	9	10	
15	16	17	
22	23	24	
29	30	31 HALLOWEEN	

WEEKLY FOOD DIARY

	MONDAY	TUESDAY	WEDNESDAY	THURSDAY	FRIDAY	SATURDAY	SUNDAY
DAILY TOTALS	MILK FAT PROTEIN VEG BREAD FRUIT	MILK FAT PROTEIN VEG BREAD FRUIT	MILK FAT PROTEIN VEG BREAD FRUIT	MILK FAT PROTEIN VEG BREAD FRUIT	MILK FAT PROTEIN VEG BREAD FRUIT	MILK FAT PROTEIN VEG BREAD FRUIT	MILK FAT PROTEIN VEG BREAD FRUIT
BREAKFAST							
LUNCH							
DINNER							
SNACKS							

WEEKLY LIMITS EGGS/ORGAN MEAT _____ CHEESE/MEAT _____ FLOATER℠ _____ OPTIONAL CALORIES _____

I will attend my Weight Watchers meeting this week on _____

SEPTEMBER / OCTOBER 1992

GOAL:

MONDAY 28 / FIRST DAY OF ROSH HASHANAH

TUESDAY 29

WEDNESDAY 30

THURSDAY 1

FRIDAY 2

SATURDAY 3 / SUNDAY 4

To help with weight-loss ups and downs, a group of us created a buddy system; just pick up the phone and call a fellow member when you're having a bad day.

—Celeste N. Gibala

WEEKLY FOOD DIARY

	MONDAY	TUESDAY	WEDNESDAY	THURSDAY	FRIDAY	SATURDAY	SUNDAY
DAILY TOTALS	MILK ____ FAT ____ PROTEIN ____ VEG ____ BREAD ____ FRUIT ____	MILK ____ FAT ____ PROTEIN ____ VEG ____ BREAD ____ FRUIT ____	MILK ____ FAT ____ PROTEIN ____ VEG ____ BREAD ____ FRUIT ____	MILK ____ FAT ____ PROTEIN ____ VEG ____ BREAD ____ FRUIT ____	MILK ____ FAT ____ PROTEIN ____ VEG ____ BREAD ____ FRUIT ____	MILK ____ FAT ____ PROTEIN ____ VEG ____ BREAD ____ FRUIT ____	MILK ____ FAT ____ PROTEIN ____ VEG ____ BREAD ____ FRUIT ____
BREAKFAST							
LUNCH							
DINNER							
SNACKS							

WEEKLY LIMITS EGGS/ORGAN MEAT _____ CHEESE/MEAT _____ FLOATER® _____

I will attend my Weight Watchers meeting this week on _____ OPTIONAL CALORIES _____

OCTOBER 1992

GOAL :

MONDAY 5

TUESDAY 6

WEDNESDAY 7 / YOM KIPPUR

THURSDAY 8

FRIDAY 9

SATURDAY 10 / SUNDAY 11

You need a plan to handle yourself in those situations when, in the past, your first response was to eat. By thinking and practicing in your mind new and better ways to react, you'll be prepared and you'll be in control.

WEEKLY FOOD DIARY

	MONDAY	TUESDAY	WEDNESDAY	THURSDAY	FRIDAY	SATURDAY	SUNDAY
DAILY TOTALS	MILK FAT PROTEIN VEG BREAD FRUIT	MILK FAT PROTEIN VEG BREAD FRUIT	MILK FAT PROTEIN VEG BREAD FRUIT	MILK FAT PROTEIN VEG BREAD FRUIT	MILK FAT PROTEIN VEG BREAD FRUIT	MILK FAT PROTEIN VEG BREAD FRUIT	MILK FAT PROTEIN VEG BREAD FRUIT
BREAKFAST							
LUNCH							
DINNER							
SNACKS							

WEEKLY LIMITS EGGS/ORGAN MEAT _____ CHEESE/MEAT _____ FLOATER®

OPTIONAL CALORIES

I will attend my Weight Watchers meeting this week on _____

OCTOBER 1992

WEIGHT WATCHERS

GOAL:

MONDAY 12 / COLUMBUS DAY

TUESDAY 13

WEDNESDAY 14

THURSDAY 15

FRIDAY 16

SATURDAY 17 / SUNDAY 18

I have learned that food does not control my life, but that I am in control.
This is a whole new way of thinking for me.

—*Jeffrey Hacker*

WEEKLY FOOD DIARY

	MONDAY	TUESDAY	WEDNESDAY	THURSDAY	FRIDAY	SATURDAY	SUNDAY
DAILY TOTALS	MILK ___ FAT ___ PROTEIN ___ VEG ___ BREAD ___ FRUIT ___	MILK ___ FAT ___ PROTEIN ___ VEG ___ BREAD ___ FRUIT ___	MILK ___ FAT ___ PROTEIN ___ VEG ___ BREAD ___ FRUIT ___	MILK ___ FAT ___ PROTEIN ___ VEG ___ BREAD ___ FRUIT ___	MILK ___ FAT ___ PROTEIN ___ VEG ___ BREAD ___ FRUIT ___	MILK ___ FAT ___ PROTEIN ___ VEG ___ BREAD ___ FRUIT ___	MILK ___ FAT ___ PROTEIN ___ VEG ___ BREAD ___ FRUIT ___
BREAKFAST							
LUNCH							
DINNER							
SNACKS							

WEEKLY LIMITS EGGS/ORGAN MEAT ___ CHEESE/MEAT ___

FLOATER®

OPTIONAL CALORIES

I will attend my Weight Watchers meeting this week on ___

OCTOBER 1992

GOAL:

MONDAY 19

TUESDAY 20

WEDNESDAY 21

THURSDAY 22

FRIDAY 23

SATURDAY 24 / SUNDAY 25 / DST ENDS

Don't skip dinner because you are trying to lose weight. If dining out with a group, be the first to order. You'll be less swayed by other people's choices.

W E E K L Y   F O O D   D I A R Y

	MONDAY	TUESDAY	WEDNESDAY	THURSDAY	FRIDAY	SATURDAY	SUNDAY
DAILY TOTALS	MILK ___ FAT ___ PROTEIN ___ VEG ___ BREAD ___ FRUIT ___	MILK ___ FAT ___ PROTEIN ___ VEG ___ BREAD ___ FRUIT ___	MILK ___ FAT ___ PROTEIN ___ VEG ___ BREAD ___ FRUIT ___	MILK ___ FAT ___ PROTEIN ___ VEG ___ BREAD ___ FRUIT ___	MILK ___ FAT ___ PROTEIN ___ VEG ___ BREAD ___ FRUIT ___	MILK ___ FAT ___ PROTEIN ___ VEG ___ BREAD ___ FRUIT ___	MILK ___ FAT ___ PROTEIN ___ VEG ___ BREAD ___ FRUIT ___
BREAKFAST							
LUNCH							
DINNER							
SNACKS							

WEEKLY LIMITS EGGS/ORGAN MEAT _____ CHEESE/MEAT _____ FLOATER® _____

OPTIONAL CALORIES _____

I will attend my Weight Watchers meeting this week on _____

OCTOBER / NOVEMBER 1992

GOAL:

MONDAY 26

TUESDAY 27

WEDNESDAY 28

THURSDAY 29

FRIDAY 30

SATURDAY 31 / HALLOWEEN / SUNDAY 1

Think positively; even if you mess up one day, just start fresh the next morning.

—Claire Trapp

NOVEMBER 1992

SUNDAY	MONDAY	TUESDAY	WEDNESDAY
1	2	3 ELECTION DAY	4
8	9	10	11 VETERANS DAY
15	16	17	18
22	23	24	25
29	30		

NOVEMBER 1992

THURSDAY	FRIDAY	SATURDAY	NOTES
5	6	7	
12	13	14	
19	20	21	
26 THANKSGIVING	27	28	

WEEKLY FOOD DIARY

	MONDAY	TUESDAY	WEDNESDAY	THURSDAY	FRIDAY	SATURDAY	SUNDAY
DAILY TOTALS	MILK FAT PROTEIN VEG BREAD FRUIT	MILK FAT PROTEIN VEG BREAD FRUIT	MILK FAT PROTEIN VEG BREAD FRUIT	MILK FAT PROTEIN VEG BREAD FRUIT	MILK FAT PROTEIN VEG BREAD FRUIT	MILK FAT PROTEIN VEG BREAD FRUIT	MILK FAT PROTEIN VEG BREAD FRUIT
BREAKFAST							
LUNCH							
DINNER							
SNACKS							

WEEKLY LIMITS EGGS/ORGAN MEAT _____ CHEESE/MEAT _____

FLOATER®

I will attend my Weight Watchers meeting this week on _____

OPTIONAL CALORIES

NOVEMBER 1992

WEIGHT WATCHERS

GOAL:

MONDAY 2

TUESDAY 3 / ELECTION DAY

WEDNESDAY 4

THURSDAY 5

FRIDAY 6

SATURDAY 7 / SUNDAY 8

Make smart shopping a part of your action plan. Always make a list. You'll be less tempted to buy snacks if you shop prepared. Keep the plan of your supermarket in mind, and make your list up aisle by aisle.

W E E K L Y   F O O D   D I A R Y

	MONDAY	TUESDAY	WEDNESDAY	THURSDAY	FRIDAY	SATURDAY	SUNDAY
DAILY TOTALS	MILK FAT PROTEIN VEG BREAD FRUIT	MILK FAT PROTEIN VEG BREAD FRUIT	MILK FAT PROTEIN VEG BREAD FRUIT	MILK FAT PROTEIN VEG BREAD FRUIT	MILK FAT PROTEIN VEG BREAD FRUIT	MILK FAT PROTEIN VEG BREAD FRUIT	MILK FAT PROTEIN VEG BREAD FRUIT
BREAKFAST							
LUNCH							
DINNER							
SNACKS							

WEEKLY LIMITS EGGS/ORGAN MEAT _____ CHEESE/MEAT _____ FLOATER™ _____

OPTIONAL CALORIES

I will attend my Weight Watchers meeting this week on _____

NOVEMBER 1992

WEIGHT WATCHERS

GOAL:

MONDAY 9

TUESDAY 10

WEDNESDAY 11 / VETERANS DAY

THURSDAY 12

FRIDAY 13

SATURDAY 14 / SUNDAY 15

Water, water, water. And, write it down; it's very easy to lose track. All the hard work pays off.

—Paula Falconio

WEEKLY FOOD DIARY

	MONDAY	TUESDAY	WEDNESDAY	THURSDAY	FRIDAY	SATURDAY	SUNDAY
DAILY TOTALS	MILK FAT PROTEIN VEG BREAD FRUIT	MILK FAT PROTEIN VEG BREAD FRUIT	MILK FAT PROTEIN VEG BREAD FRUIT	MILK FAT PROTEIN VEG BREAD FRUIT	MILK FAT PROTEIN VEG BREAD FRUIT	MILK FAT PROTEIN VEG BREAD FRUIT	MILK FAT PROTEIN VEG BREAD FRUIT
BREAKFAST							
LUNCH							
DINNER							
SNACKS							

WEEKLY LIMITS EGGS/ORGAN MEAT _____ CHEESE/MEAT _____

FLOATER®

OPTIONAL CALORIES

I will attend my Weight Watchers meeting this week on _____

NOVEMBER 1992

WEIGHT WATCHERS

GOAL:

MONDAY 16

TUESDAY 17

WEDNESDAY 18

THURSDAY 19

FRIDAY 20

SATURDAY 21 / SUNDAY 22

The key to success is to be positive. Imagine yourself carrying out your weight-loss plan. It feels great to take steps to reach your goal. It feels even better to lose weight and look thinner. Remember these good feelings and keep this positive image in your mind.

WEEKLY FOOD DIARY

	MONDAY	TUESDAY	WEDNESDAY	THURSDAY	FRIDAY	SATURDAY	SUNDAY		
DAILY TOTALS	MILK __ FAT __ PROTEIN __ VEG __ BREAD __ FRUIT __		MILK __ FAT __ PROTEIN __ VEG __ BREAD __ FRUIT __		MILK __ FAT __ PROTEIN __ VEG __ BREAD __ FRUIT __		MILK __ FAT __ PROTEIN __ VEG __ BREAD __ FRUIT __		
BREAKFAST									
LUNCH									
DINNER									
SNACKS									

WEEKLY LIMITS EGGS/ORGAN MEAT _____ CHEESE/MEAT _____ FLOATER®

I will attend my Weight Watchers meeting this week on _____ OPTIONAL CALORIES

NOVEMBER 1992

GOAL:

MONDAY 23

TUESDAY 24

WEDNESDAY 25

THURSDAY 26 / THANKSGIVING

FRIDAY 27

SATURDAY 28 / SUNDAY 29

If you're invited to a dinner party, call ahead, ask about the menu, and plan your day around it.

DECEMBER 1992

SUNDAY	MONDAY	TUESDAY	WEDNESDAY
		1	2
6	7	8	9
13	14	15	16
20 FIRST DAY OF HANUKKAH	21	22	23
27	28	29	30

DECEMBER 1992

THURSDAY	FRIDAY	SATURDAY	NOTES
3	4	5	
10	11	12	
17	18	19	
24	25 CHRISTMAS	26	
31			

WEEKLY FOOD DIARY

	MONDAY	TUESDAY	WEDNESDAY	THURSDAY	FRIDAY	SATURDAY	SUNDAY
DAILY	MILK ___ FAT ___ PROTEIN ___ VEG ___ BREAD ___ FRUIT ___	MILK ___ FAT ___ PROTEIN ___ VEG ___ BREAD ___ FRUIT ___	MILK ___ FAT ___ PROTEIN ___ VEG ___ BREAD ___ FRUIT ___	MILK ___ FAT ___ PROTEIN ___ VEG ___ BREAD ___ FRUIT ___	MILK ___ FAT ___ PROTEIN ___ VEG ___ BREAD ___ FRUIT ___	MILK ___ FAT ___ PROTEIN ___ VEG ___ BREAD ___ FRUIT ___	MILK ___ FAT ___ PROTEIN ___ VEG ___ BREAD ___ FRUIT ___
BREAKFAST							
LUNCH							
DINNER							
SNACKS							

WEEKLY LIMITS EGGS/ORGAN MEAT ___ CHEESE/MEAT ___ FLOATER®___

OPTIONAL CALORIES ___

I will attend my Weight Watchers meeting this week on ___

NOVEMBER / DECEMBER 1992

GOAL:

MONDAY 30

TUESDAY 1

WEDNESDAY 2

THURSDAY 3

FRIDAY 4

SATURDAY 5 / SUNDAY 6

I notice that when I acquire a discipline in my food intake, this discipline carries over to other parts of my life.

—Josephine Grimaldi

WEEKLY FOOD DIARY

	MONDAY	TUESDAY	WEDNESDAY	THURSDAY	FRIDAY	SATURDAY	SUNDAY
TO-TAL-LYS	MILK ___ FAT ___ PROTEIN ___ VEG ___ BREAD ___ FRUIT ___	MILK ___ FAT ___ PROTEIN ___ VEG ___ BREAD ___ FRUIT ___	MILK ___ FAT ___ PROTEIN ___ VEG ___ BREAD ___ FRUIT ___	MILK ___ FAT ___ PROTEIN ___ VEG ___ BREAD ___ FRUIT ___	MILK ___ FAT ___ PROTEIN ___ VEG ___ BREAD ___ FRUIT ___	MILK ___ FAT ___ PROTEIN ___ VEG ___ BREAD ___ FRUIT ___	MILK ___ FAT ___ PROTEIN ___ VEG ___ BREAD ___ FRUIT ___
BREAKFAST							
LUNCH							
DINNER							
SNACKS							

WEEKLY LIMITS EGGS/ORGAN MEAT _____ CHEESE/MEAT _____ FLOATER® _____

I will attend my Weight Watchers meeting this week on _____ OPTIONAL CALORIES _____

DECEMBER 1992

GOAL:

MONDAY 7

TUESDAY 8

WEDNESDAY 9

THURSDAY 10

FRIDAY 11

SATURDAY 12 / SUNDAY 13

Add variety to your low-calorie snacks by choosing foods with satisfying flavors and textures: dried unsweetened fruit chips (made without oil), crunchy raw vegetables, air-popped popcorn with herb seasoning, and rice-cake snacks. Rather than chips and dip, try raw vegetables with salsa.

WEEKLY FOOD DIARY

	MONDAY	TUESDAY	WEDNESDAY	THURSDAY	FRIDAY	SATURDAY	SUNDAY
DAILY TOTALS	MILK ___ FAT ___ PROTEIN ___ VEG ___ BREAD ___ FRUIT ___	MILK ___ FAT ___ PROTEIN ___ VEG ___ BREAD ___ FRUIT ___	MILK ___ FAT ___ PROTEIN ___ VEG ___ BREAD ___ FRUIT ___	MILK ___ FAT ___ PROTEIN ___ VEG ___ BREAD ___ FRUIT ___	MILK ___ FAT ___ PROTEIN ___ VEG ___ BREAD ___ FRUIT ___	MILK ___ FAT ___ PROTEIN ___ VEG ___ BREAD ___ FRUIT ___	MILK ___ FAT ___ PROTEIN ___ VEG ___ BREAD ___ FRUIT ___
BREAKFAST							
LUNCH							
DINNER							
SNACKS							

WEEKLY LIMITS EGGS/ORGAN MEAT _____ CHEESE/MEAT _____

FLOATER®

OPTIONAL CALORIES

I will attend my Weight Watchers meeting this week on _____

DECEMBER 1992

WEIGHT WATCHERS

GOAL:

MONDAY 14

TUESDAY 15

WEDNESDAY 16

THURSDAY 17

FRIDAY 18

SATURDAY 19 / SUNDAY 20 / FIRST DAY OF HANUKKAH

My success has always been around the corner and I didn't know it; I only knew the other side. Now I have more self-esteem and self-confidence than ever before in my life.

—Vicky Wolbert

WEEKLY FOOD DIARY

	MONDAY	TUESDAY	WEDNESDAY	THURSDAY	FRIDAY	SATURDAY	SUNDAY
DAILY TOTALS	MILK___ FAT___ PROTEIN___ VEG___ BREAD___ FRUIT___		MILK___ FAT___ PROTEIN___ VEG___ BREAD___ FRUIT___	MILK___ FAT___ PROTEIN___ VEG___ BREAD___ FRUIT___	MILK___ FAT___ PROTEIN___ VEG___ BREAD___ FRUIT___	MILK___ FAT___ PROTEIN___ VEG___ BREAD___ FRUIT___	MILK___ FAT___ PROTEIN___ VEG___ BREAD___ FRUIT___
BREAKFAST							
LUNCH							
DINNER							
SNACKS							

WEEKLY LIMITS EGGS/ORGAN MEAT _____ CHEESE/MEAT _____ FLOATER® _____

OPTIONAL CALORIES _____

I will attend my Weight Watchers meeting this week on _____

DECEMBER 1992

GOAL:

MONDAY 21

TUESDAY 22

WEDNESDAY 23

THURSDAY 24

FRIDAY 25 / CHRISTMAS

SATURDAY 26 / SUNDAY 27

If you're attending a party, don't arrive hungry. If you have a snack before you leave, you'll be less likely to overeat. Once at the party, look for items like raw vegetables and fruits. If you want to splurge on an alcoholic beverage, try a white wine spritzer.

JANUARY 1993

SUNDAY	MONDAY	TUESDAY	WEDNESDAY
3	4	5	6
10	11	12	13
17	18 DR. MARTIN LUTHER KING, JR.'S BIRTHDAY (OBSERVED)	19	20
24 31	25	26	27

JANUARY 1993

THURSDAY	FRIDAY	SATURDAY	NOTES
	1 NEW YEAR'S DAY	2	
7	8	9	
14	15 DR. MARTIN LUTHER KING, JR.'S BIRTHDAY	16	
21	22	23	
28	29	30	

WEEKLY FOOD DIARY

	MONDAY	TUESDAY	WEDNESDAY	THURSDAY	FRIDAY	SATURDAY	SUNDAY
DAILY TOTALS	MILK FAT PROTEIN VEG BREAD FRUIT	MILK FAT PROTEIN VEG BREAD FRUIT	MILK FAT PROTEIN VEG BREAD FRUIT	MILK FAT PROTEIN VEG BREAD FRUIT	MILK FAT PROTEIN VEG BREAD FRUIT	MILK FAT PROTEIN VEG BREAD FRUIT	MILK FAT PROTEIN VEG BREAD FRUIT
BREAKFAST							
LUNCH							
DINNER							
SNACKS							

WEEKLY LIMITS EGGS/ORGAN MEAT _____ CHEESE/MEAT _____ FLOATER® _____

OPTIONAL CALORIES _____

I will attend my Weight Watchers meeting this week on _____

DECEMBER / JANUARY 1992 – 93

GOAL :

MONDAY 28

TUESDAY 29

WEDNESDAY 30

THURSDAY 31

FRIDAY 1 / NEW YEAR'S DAY

SATURDAY 2 / SUNDAY 3

Write it all down and take one day at a time. Remember, no one is perfect and that's OK.

—Linda Fleming

WEEKLY FOOD DIARY

	MONDAY	TUESDAY	WEDNESDAY	THURSDAY	FRIDAY	SATURDAY	SUNDAY
DAILY TOTALS	MILK ___ FAT ___ PROTEIN ___ VEG ___ BREAD ___ FRUIT ___	MILK ___ FAT ___ PROTEIN ___ VEG ___ BREAD ___ FRUIT ___	MILK ___ FAT ___ PROTEIN ___ VEG ___ BREAD ___ FRUIT ___	MILK ___ FAT ___ PROTEIN ___ VEG ___ BREAD ___ FRUIT ___	MILK ___ FAT ___ PROTEIN ___ VEG ___ BREAD ___ FRUIT ___	MILK ___ FAT ___ PROTEIN ___ VEG ___ BREAD ___ FRUIT ___	MILK ___ FAT ___ PROTEIN ___ VEG ___ BREAD ___ FRUIT ___
BREAKFAST							
LUNCH							
DINNER							
SNACKS							

FLOATER®

WEEKLY LIMITS EGGS/ORGAN MEAT _____ CHEESE/MEAT _____

OPTIONAL CALORIES _____

I will attend my Weight Watchers meeting this week on _____

JANUARY 1993

GOAL:

MONDAY 4

TUESDAY 5

WEDNESDAY 6

THURSDAY 7

FRIDAY 8

SATURDAY 9 / SUNDAY 10

You've made a choice to look and feel better in 1993—and you're going to do it!

WEEKLY FOOD DIARY

	MONDAY	TUESDAY	WEDNESDAY	THURSDAY	FRIDAY	SATURDAY	SUNDAY
DAILY TOTALS	MILK FAT PROTEIN VEG BREAD FRUIT	MILK FAT PROTEIN VEG BREAD FRUIT	MILK FAT PROTEIN VEG BREAD FRUIT	MILK FAT PROTEIN VEG BREAD FRUIT	MILK FAT PROTEIN VEG BREAD FRUIT	MILK FAT PROTEIN VEG BREAD FRUIT	MILK FAT PROTEIN VEG BREAD FRUIT
BREAKFAST							
LUNCH							
DINNER							
SNACKS							

WEEKLY LIMITS EGGS/ORGAN MEAT _____ CHEESE/MEAT _____ FLOATER® _____

OPTIONAL CALORIES

I will attend my Weight Watchers meeting this week on _____

JANUARY 1993

WEIGHT WATCHERS

GOAL:

MONDAY 11

TUESDAY 12

WEDNESDAY 13

THURSDAY 14

FRIDAY 15 / DR. MARTIN LUTHER KING, JR.'S BIRTHDAY

SATURDAY 16 / SUNDAY 17

I set big and little goals and work toward them. Failure is not failure unless we let it be. So each day I strive to reach those goals, then I set new ones. Now I look back and know that I have done my best.

—Jean A. Rawson

WEEKLY FOOD DIARY

	MONDAY	TUESDAY	WEDNESDAY	THURSDAY	FRIDAY	SATURDAY	SUNDAY
DAILY TOTALS	MILK____ FAT____ PROTEIN____ VEG____ BREAD____ FRUIT____	MILK____ FAT____ PROTEIN____ VEG____ BREAD____ FRUIT____	MILK____ FAT____ PROTEIN____ VEG____ BREAD____ FRUIT____	MILK____ FAT____ PROTEIN____ VEG____ BREAD____ FRUIT____	MILK____ FAT____ PROTEIN____ VEG____ BREAD____ FRUIT____	MILK____ FAT____ PROTEIN____ VEG____ BREAD____ FRUIT____	MILK____ FAT____ PROTEIN____ VEG____ BREAD____ FRUIT____
BREAKFAST							
LUNCH							
DINNER							
SNACKS							

WEEKLY LIMITS EGGS/ORGAN MEAT _____ CHEESE/MEAT _____ FLOATER® _____ OPTIONAL CALORIES _____

I will attend my Weight Watchers meeting this week on _____

JANUARY 1993

WEIGHT WATCHERS

GOAL:

MONDAY 18 / DR. MARTIN LUTHER KING, JR.'S BIRTHDAY (OBSERVED)

TUESDAY 19

WEDNESDAY 20

THURSDAY 21

FRIDAY 22

SATURDAY 23 / SUNDAY 24

Remember that any decision not to eat a tempting food is a choice—a choice that will help you achieve your goal.

WEEKLY FOOD DIARY

	MONDAY	TUESDAY	WEDNESDAY	THURSDAY	FRIDAY	SATURDAY	SUNDAY
DAILY TOTALS	MILK ___ FAT ___ PROTEIN ___ VEG ___ BREAD ___ FRUIT ___	MILK ___ FAT ___ PROTEIN ___ VEG ___ BREAD ___ FRUIT ___	MILK ___ FAT ___ PROTEIN ___ VEG ___ BREAD ___ FRUIT ___	MILK ___ FAT ___ PROTEIN ___ VEG ___ BREAD ___ FRUIT ___	MILK ___ FAT ___ PROTEIN ___ VEG ___ BREAD ___ FRUIT ___	MILK ___ FAT ___ PROTEIN ___ VEG ___ BREAD ___ FRUIT ___	MILK ___ FAT ___ PROTEIN ___ VEG ___ BREAD ___ FRUIT ___
BREAKFAST							
LUNCH							
DINNER							
SNACKS							

WEEKLY LIMITS EGGS/ORGAN MEAT ___ CHEESE/MEAT ___

FLOATER®

OPTIONAL CALORIES ___

I will attend my Weight Watchers meeting this week on ___

JANUARY 1993

WEIGHT WATCHERS

GOAL:

MONDAY 25

TUESDAY 26

WEDNESDAY 27

THURSDAY 28

FRIDAY 29

SATURDAY 30 / SUNDAY 31

It's not easy, and there will be feelings of frustration, but the best way to conquer them is to remember your objectives and keep yourself in a positive frame of mind.

—*Lynn Yonren*

FEBRUARY 1993

SUNDAY	MONDAY	TUESDAY	WEDNESDAY
	1	2	3
7	8	9	10
14 VALENTINE'S DAY	15 PRESIDENTS' DAY	16	17
21	22	23	24
28			

FEBRUARY 1993

THURSDAY	FRIDAY	SATURDAY	NOTES
4	5	6	
11	12	13	
18	19	20	
25	26	27	

WEEKLY FOOD DIARY

	MONDAY	TUESDAY	WEDNESDAY	THURSDAY	FRIDAY	SATURDAY	SUNDAY
DAILY TOTALS	MILK ___ FAT ___ PROTEIN ___ VEG ___ BREAD ___ FRUIT ___	MILK ___ FAT ___ PROTEIN ___ VEG ___ BREAD ___ FRUIT ___	MILK ___ FAT ___ PROTEIN ___ VEG ___ BREAD ___ FRUIT ___	MILK ___ FAT ___ PROTEIN ___ VEG ___ BREAD ___ FRUIT ___	MILK ___ FAT ___ PROTEIN ___ VEG ___ BREAD ___ FRUIT ___	MILK ___ FAT ___ PROTEIN ___ VEG ___ BREAD ___ FRUIT ___	MILK ___ FAT ___ PROTEIN ___ VEG ___ BREAD ___ FRUIT ___
BREAKFAST							
LUNCH							
DINNER							
SNACKS							

WEEKLY LIMITS EGGS/ORGAN MEAT ___ CHEESE/MEAT ___

I will attend my Weight Watchers meeting this week on ___

FLOATER®

OPTIONAL CALORIES

FEBRUARY 1993

GOAL:

MONDAY 1

TUESDAY 2

WEDNESDAY 3

THURSDAY 4

FRIDAY 5

SATURDAY 6 / SUNDAY 7

If you want to reach your goal—walk to it! Walking is easy, costs nothing, and you can do it anywhere. If you make no other changes, but walk briskly each day, you'll reach your goal before you know it.

WEEKLY FOOD DIARY

	MONDAY	TUESDAY	WEDNESDAY	THURSDAY	FRIDAY	SATURDAY	SUNDAY
DAILY TOTALS	MILK ___ FAT ___ PROTEIN ___ VEG ___ BREAD ___ FRUIT ___	MILK ___ FAT ___ PROTEIN ___ VEG ___ BREAD ___ FRUIT ___	MILK ___ FAT ___ PROTEIN ___ VEG ___ BREAD ___ FRUIT ___	MILK ___ FAT ___ PROTEIN ___ VEG ___ BREAD ___ FRUIT ___	MILK ___ FAT ___ PROTEIN ___ VEG ___ BREAD ___ FRUIT ___	MILK ___ FAT ___ PROTEIN ___ VEG ___ BREAD ___ FRUIT ___	MILK ___ FAT ___ PROTEIN ___ VEG ___ BREAD ___ FRUIT ___
BREAKFAST							
LUNCH							
DINNER							
SNACKS							

WEEKLY LIMITS EGGS/ORGAN MEAT _____ CHEESE/MEAT _____ FLOATER® _____

OPTIONAL CALORIES _____

I will attend my Weight Watchers meeting this week on _____

FEBRUARY 1993

WEIGHT WATCHERS

GOAL:

MONDAY 8

TUESDAY 9

WEDNESDAY 10

THURSDAY 11

FRIDAY 12

SATURDAY 13 / SUNDAY 14 / VALENTINE'S DAY

Family support was the key for me. Recently my husband traveled to Hershey, Pennsylvania. Yikes, I thought, he always brings me a gift. Talk about supportive! This year he brought me cocoa-butter bath soap.

—*Marsha Forsey*

WEEKLY FOOD DIARY

	MONDAY	TUESDAY	WEDNESDAY	THURSDAY	FRIDAY	SATURDAY	SUNDAY
DAILY TOTALS	MILK ___ FAT ___ PROTEIN ___ VEG ___ BREAD ___ FRUIT ___	MILK ___ FAT ___ PROTEIN ___ VEG ___ BREAD ___ FRUIT ___	MILK ___ FAT ___ PROTEIN ___ VEG ___ BREAD ___ FRUIT ___	MILK ___ FAT ___ PROTEIN ___ VEG ___ BREAD ___ FRUIT ___	MILK ___ FAT ___ PROTEIN ___ VEG ___ BREAD ___ FRUIT ___	MILK ___ FAT ___ PROTEIN ___ VEG ___ BREAD ___ FRUIT ___	MILK ___ FAT ___ PROTEIN ___ VEG ___ BREAD ___ FRUIT ___
BREAKFAST							
LUNCH							
DINNER							
SNACKS							

WEEKLY LIMITS EGGS/ORGAN MEAT _____ CHEESE/MEAT _____

FLOATER®

OPTIONAL CALORIES

I will attend my Weight Watchers meeting this week on _____

FEBRUARY 1993

GOAL :

MONDAY 15 / PRESIDENTS' DAY

TUESDAY 16

WEDNESDAY 17

THURSDAY 18

FRIDAY 19

SATURDAY 20 / SUNDAY 21

As each day of my weight-loss program progresses, I feel a certain tingle. There is a glow on my face, people are complimenting me, and I walk with confidence.

—Yvonne Molloy

WEEKLY FOOD DIARY

	MONDAY	TUESDAY	WEDNESDAY	THURSDAY	FRIDAY	SATURDAY	SUNDAY
DAILY TOTALS	MILK FAT PROTEIN VEG BREAD FRUIT	MILK FAT PROTEIN VEG BREAD FRUIT	MILK FAT PROTEIN VEG BREAD FRUIT	MILK FAT PROTEIN VEG BREAD FRUIT	MILK FAT PROTEIN VEG BREAD FRUIT	MILK FAT PROTEIN VEG BREAD FRUIT	MILK FAT PROTEIN VEG BREAD FRUIT
BREAKFAST							
LUNCH							
DINNER							
SNACKS							

WEEKLY LIMITS EGGS/ORGAN MEAT _____ CHEESE/MEAT _____ FLOATER® _____

I will attend my Weight Watchers meeting this week on _____ OPTIONAL CALORIES _____

FEBRUARY 1993

GOAL:

MONDAY 22

TUESDAY 23

WEDNESDAY 24

THURSDAY 25

FRIDAY 26

SATURDAY 27 / SUNDAY 28

For successful weight control, take twenty—twenty minutes for your stomach to tell you that you're full.

MARCH 1993

SUNDAY	MONDAY	TUESDAY	WEDNESDAY
	1	2	3
7	8	9	10
14	15	16	17 ST. PATRICK'S DAY
21	22	23	24
28	29	30	31

MARCH 1993

THURSDAY	FRIDAY	SATURDAY	NOTES
4	5	6	
11	12	13	
18	19	20	
25	26	27	

WEEKLY FOOD DIARY

	MONDAY	TUESDAY	WEDNESDAY	THURSDAY	FRIDAY	SATURDAY	SUNDAY
DAILY TOTALS	MILK FAT PROTEIN VEG BREAD FRUIT	MILK FAT PROTEIN VEG BREAD FRUIT	MILK FAT PROTEIN VEG BREAD FRUIT	MILK FAT PROTEIN VEG BREAD FRUIT	MILK FAT PROTEIN VEG BREAD FRUIT	MILK FAT PROTEIN VEG BREAD FRUIT	MILK FAT PROTEIN VEG BREAD FRUIT
BREAKFAST							
LUNCH							
DINNER							
SNACKS							

WEEKLY LIMITS EGGS/ORGAN MEAT _____ CHEESE/MEAT _____ FLOATER® _____

OPTIONAL CALORIES _____

I will attend my Weight Watchers meeting this week on _____

MARCH 1993

GOAL:

MONDAY 1

TUESDAY 2

WEDNESDAY 3

THURSDAY 4

FRIDAY 5

SATURDAY 6 / SUNDAY 7

I have finally accepted responsibility for my success or failure; before, I only accepted failure. Now, I don't give in or give up; I'm proud to be on the road to success.

—*Carolyn F. Grain*

WEEKLY FOOD DIARY

	MONDAY	TUESDAY	WEDNESDAY	THURSDAY	FRIDAY	SATURDAY	SUNDAY
DAILY TOTALS	MILK FAT PROTEIN VEG BREAD FRUIT	MILK FAT PROTEIN VEG BREAD FRUIT	MILK FAT PROTEIN VEG BREAD FRUIT	MILK FAT PROTEIN VEG BREAD FRUIT	MILK FAT PROTEIN VEG BREAD FRUIT	MILK FAT PROTEIN VEG BREAD FRUIT	MILK FAT PROTEIN VEG BREAD FRUIT
BREAKFAST							
LUNCH							
DINNER							
SNACKS							

FLOATER®

OPTIONAL CALORIES

WEEKLY LIMITS EGGS/ORGAN MEAT _____ CHEESE/MEAT _____

I will attend my Weight Watchers meeting this week on _____

MARCH 1993

GOAL:

MONDAY 8

TUESDAY 9

WEDNESDAY 10

THURSDAY 11

FRIDAY 12

SATURDAY 13 / SUNDAY 14

Try to put down your fork between bites. Chew and swallow before you put more food in your mouth.

If you've finished with your meal in less than twenty minutes, wait ten more before having dessert.

W E E K L Y   F O O D   D I A R Y

	MONDAY	TUESDAY	WEDNESDAY	THURSDAY	FRIDAY	SATURDAY	SUNDAY
DAILY TOTALS	MILK ___ FAT ___ PROTEIN ___ VEG ___ BREAD ___ FRUIT ___	MILK ___ FAT ___ PROTEIN ___ VEG ___ BREAD ___ FRUIT ___	MILK ___ FAT ___ PROTEIN ___ VEG ___ BREAD ___ FRUIT ___	MILK ___ FAT ___ PROTEIN ___ VEG ___ BREAD ___ FRUIT ___	MILK ___ FAT ___ PROTEIN ___ VEG ___ BREAD ___ FRUIT ___	MILK ___ FAT ___ PROTEIN ___ VEG ___ BREAD ___ FRUIT ___	MILK ___ FAT ___ PROTEIN ___ VEG ___ BREAD ___ FRUIT ___
BREAKFAST							
LUNCH							
DINNER							
SNACKS							

WEEKLY LIMITS EGGS/ORGAN MEAT _____ CHEESE/MEAT _____ FLOATER® _____

I will attend my Weight Watchers meeting this week on _____ OPTIONAL CALORIES _____

MARCH 1993

GOAL:

MONDAY 15

TUESDAY 16

WEDNESDAY 17 / ST. PATRICK'S DAY

THURSDAY 18

FRIDAY 19

SATURDAY 20 / SUNDAY 21

Delay tactics help me; I walk, take a bath, or write a letter when I feel out of control.

—Sheila Josephson

WEEKLY FOOD DIARY

	MONDAY	TUESDAY	WEDNESDAY	THURSDAY	FRIDAY	SATURDAY	SUNDAY
DAILY TOTALS	MILK ___ FAT ___ PROTEIN ___ VEG ___ BREAD ___ FRUIT ___	MILK ___ FAT ___ PROTEIN ___ VEG ___ BREAD ___ FRUIT ___	MILK ___ FAT ___ PROTEIN ___ VEG ___ BREAD ___ FRUIT ___	MILK ___ FAT ___ PROTEIN ___ VEG ___ BREAD ___ FRUIT ___	MILK ___ FAT ___ PROTEIN ___ VEG ___ BREAD ___ FRUIT ___	MILK ___ FAT ___ PROTEIN ___ VEG ___ BREAD ___ FRUIT ___	MILK ___ FAT ___ PROTEIN ___ VEG ___ BREAD ___ FRUIT ___
BREAKFAST							
LUNCH							
DINNER							
SNACKS							

WEEKLY LIMITS EGGS/ORGAN MEAT _____ CHEESE/MEAT _____ FLOATER® _____

I will attend my Weight Watchers meeting this week on _____ OPTIONAL CALORIES

MARCH 1993

WEIGHT WATCHERS

GOAL:

MONDAY 22

TUESDAY 23

WEDNESDAY 24

THURSDAY 25

FRIDAY 26

SATURDAY 27 / SUNDAY 28

Make a commitment to do your eating only at the table. When you do eat, try to do nothing else except listen to music or talk with family and friends.

APRIL 1993

SUNDAY	MONDAY	TUESDAY	WEDNESDAY
4 PALM SUNDAY DST BEGINS	5	6 FIRST DAY OF PASSOVER	7
11 EASTER	12	13	14
18	19	20	21
25	26	27	28

APRIL 1993

THURSDAY	FRIDAY	SATURDAY	NOTES
1	2	3	
8	9 GOOD FRIDAY	10	
15	16	17	
22	23	24	
29	30		

WEEKLY FOOD DIARY

	MONDAY	TUESDAY	WEDNESDAY	THURSDAY	FRIDAY	SATURDAY	SUNDAY
DAILY TOTALS	MILK FAT PROTEIN VEG BREAD FRUIT	MILK FAT PROTEIN VEG BREAD FRUIT	MILK FAT PROTEIN VEG BREAD FRUIT	MILK FAT PROTEIN VEG BREAD FRUIT	MILK FAT PROTEIN VEG BREAD FRUIT	MILK FAT PROTEIN VEG BREAD FRUIT	MILK FAT PROTEIN VEG BREAD FRUIT
BREAKFAST							
LUNCH							
DINNER							
SNACKS							

WEEKLY LIMITS EGGS/ORGAN MEAT _____ CHEESE/MEAT _____ FLOATER® _____

OPTIONAL CALORIES _____

I will attend my Weight Watchers meeting this week on _____

MARCH / APRIL 1993

GOAL:

MONDAY 29

TUESDAY 30

WEDNESDAY 31

THURSDAY 1

FRIDAY 2

SATURDAY 3 / SUNDAY 4 / PALM SUNDAY / DST BEGINS

I keep a log of my daily meals and have stopped smoking for more than a year. Now I love the way I look in photographs! What next? Anything!
—*Carol A. O'Malley*

WEEKLY FOOD DIARY

	MONDAY	TUESDAY	WEDNESDAY	THURSDAY	FRIDAY	SATURDAY	SUNDAY
DAILY TOTALS	MILK — FAT — PROTEIN — VEG — BREAD — FRUIT —	MILK — FAT — PROTEIN — VEG — BREAD — FRUIT —	MILK — FAT — PROTEIN — VEG — BREAD — FRUIT —	MILK — FAT — PROTEIN — VEG — BREAD — FRUIT —	MILK — FAT — PROTEIN — VEG — BREAD — FRUIT —	MILK — FAT — PROTEIN — VEG — BREAD — FRUIT —	MILK — FAT — PROTEIN — VEG — BREAD — FRUIT —
BREAKFAST							
LUNCH							
DINNER							
SNACKS							

WEEKLY LIMITS EGGS/ORGAN MEAT _____ CHEESE/MEAT _____

FLOATER®

OPTIONAL CALORIES

I will attend my Weight Watchers meeting this week on _____

APRIL 1993

GOAL:

MONDAY 5

TUESDAY 6 / FIRST DAY OF PASSOVER

WEDNESDAY 7

THURSDAY 8

FRIDAY 9 / GOOD FRIDAY

SATURDAY 10 / SUNDAY 11 / EASTER

Whether you're at work or at home, a break in the day's schedule is a great time to recharge and relax. Take your break somewhere that you *don't* work—and don't work while you eat.

WEEKLY FOOD DIARY

	MONDAY	TUESDAY	WEDNESDAY	THURSDAY	FRIDAY	SATURDAY	SUNDAY
TOTALS	MILK FAT PROTEIN VEG BREAD FRUIT	MILK FAT PROTEIN VEG BREAD FRUIT	MILK FAT PROTEIN VEG BREAD FRUIT	MILK FAT PROTEIN VEG BREAD FRUIT	MILK FAT PROTEIN VEG BREAD FRUIT	MILK FAT PROTEIN VEG BREAD FRUIT	MILK FAT PROTEIN VEG BREAD FRUIT
BREAKFAST							
LUNCH							
DINNER							
SNACKS							

WEEKLY LIMITS EGGS/ORGAN MEAT _____ CHEESE/MEAT _____ FLOATER® _____

I will attend my Weight Watchers meeting this week on _____ OPTIONAL CALORIES _____

APRIL 1993

GOAL:

MONDAY 12

TUESDAY 13

WEDNESDAY 14

THURSDAY 15

FRIDAY 16

SATURDAY 17 / SUNDAY 18

Keep occupied. When watching television, knit, sew, write a letter, or do a crossword. Or better yet, exercise.

—*Barbara K. Swanson*

WEEKLY FOOD DIARY

	MONDAY	TUESDAY	WEDNESDAY	THURSDAY	FRIDAY	SATURDAY	SUNDAY
TOTALLYS	MILK ____ FAT ____ PROTEIN ____ VEG ____ BREAD ____ FRUIT ____	MILK ____ FAT ____ PROTEIN ____ VEG ____ BREAD ____ FRUIT ____	MILK ____ FAT ____ PROTEIN ____ VEG ____ BREAD ____ FRUIT ____	MILK ____ FAT ____ PROTEIN ____ VEG ____ BREAD ____ FRUIT ____	MILK ____ FAT ____ PROTEIN ____ VEG ____ BREAD ____ FRUIT ____	MILK ____ FAT ____ PROTEIN ____ VEG ____ BREAD ____ FRUIT ____	MILK ____ FAT ____ PROTEIN ____ VEG ____ BREAD ____ FRUIT ____
BREAKFAST							
LUNCH							
DINNER							
SNACKS							

WEEKLY LIMITS EGGS/ORGAN MEAT _____ CHEESE/MEAT _____

FLOATER® _____

OPTIONAL CALORIES _____

I will attend my Weight Watchers meeting this week on _____

APRIL 1993

GOAL :

MONDAY 19

TUESDAY 20

WEDNESDAY 21

THURSDAY 22

FRIDAY 23

SATURDAY 24 / SUNDAY 25

Physical activity is a real weight-loss booster. It burns up calories and helps you to look and feel better. Being active can also help you control negative moods that trigger overeating.

MAY 1993

SUNDAY	MONDAY	TUESDAY	WEDNESDAY
2	3	4	5
9	10	11	12
MOTHER'S DAY			
16	17	18	19
23	24	25	26
30	31		
	MEMORIAL DAY		

MAY 1993

THURSDAY	FRIDAY	SATURDAY	NOTES
		1	
6	7	8	
13	14	15	
20	21	22	
27	28	29	

WEEKLY FOOD DIARY

	MONDAY	TUESDAY	WEDNESDAY	THURSDAY	FRIDAY	SATURDAY	SUNDAY
DAILY TOTALS	MILK FAT PROTEIN VEG BREAD FRUIT	MILK FAT PROTEIN VEG BREAD FRUIT	MILK FAT PROTEIN VEG BREAD FRUIT	MILK FAT PROTEIN VEG BREAD FRUIT	MILK FAT PROTEIN VEG BREAD FRUIT	MILK FAT PROTEIN VEG BREAD FRUIT	MILK FAT PROTEIN VEG BREAD FRUIT
BREAKFAST							
LUNCH							
DINNER							
SNACKS							

WEEKLY LIMITS EGGS/ORGAN MEAT _____ CHEESE/MEAT _____ FLOATER® _____

OPTIONAL CALORIES

I will attend my Weight Watchers meeting this week on _____

APRIL / MAY 1993

WEIGHT WATCHERS

GOAL:

MONDAY 26

TUESDAY 27

WEDNESDAY 28

THURSDAY 29

FRIDAY 30

SATURDAY 1 / SUNDAY 2

I've learned to say no to overeating and to refuse seconds, and I have learned pride in moderation. I say "can do."

—Irving Gurian

WEEKLY FOOD DIARY

	MONDAY	TUESDAY	WEDNESDAY	THURSDAY	FRIDAY	SATURDAY	SUNDAY
DAILY TOTALS	MILK ___ FAT ___ PROTEIN ___ VEG ___ BREAD ___ FRUIT ___	MILK ___ FAT ___ PROTEIN ___ VEG ___ BREAD ___ FRUIT ___	MILK ___ FAT ___ PROTEIN ___ VEG ___ BREAD ___ FRUIT ___	MILK ___ FAT ___ PROTEIN ___ VEG ___ BREAD ___ FRUIT ___	MILK ___ FAT ___ PROTEIN ___ VEG ___ BREAD ___ FRUIT ___	MILK ___ FAT ___ PROTEIN ___ VEG ___ BREAD ___ FRUIT ___	MILK ___ FAT ___ PROTEIN ___ VEG ___ BREAD ___ FRUIT ___
BREAKFAST							
LUNCH							
DINNER							
SNACKS							

WEEKLY LIMITS EGGS/ORGAN MEAT _____ CHEESE/MEAT _____ FLOATER™ _____

OPTIONAL CALORIES _____

I will attend my Weight Watchers meeting this week on _____

MAY 1993

GOAL :

MONDAY 3

TUESDAY 4

WEDNESDAY 5

THURSDAY 6

FRIDAY 7

SATURDAY 8 / SUNDAY 9 / MOTHER'S DAY

Simple food changes, like substituting low-fat yogurt for mayonnaise in tuna and egg salads, have made a difference.
Moderate exercise is very important. I fitness walk.

—*Regina Walker*

WEEKLY FOOD DIARY

	MONDAY	TUESDAY	WEDNESDAY	THURSDAY	FRIDAY	SATURDAY	SUNDAY
DAILY TOTALS	MILK FAT PROTEIN VEG BREAD FRUIT	MILK FAT PROTEIN VEG BREAD FRUIT	MILK FAT PROTEIN VEG BREAD FRUIT	MILK FAT PROTEIN VEG BREAD FRUIT	MILK FAT PROTEIN VEG BREAD FRUIT	MILK FAT PROTEIN VEG BREAD FRUIT	MILK FAT PROTEIN VEG BREAD FRUIT
BREAKFAST							
LUNCH							
DINNER							
SNACKS							

WEEKLY LIMITS EGGS/ORGAN MEAT _____ CHEESE/MEAT _____

FLOATER®

OPTIONAL CALORIES

I will attend my Weight Watchers meeting this week on _____

MAY 1993

GOAL:

MONDAY 10

TUESDAY 11

WEDNESDAY 12

THURSDAY 13

FRIDAY 14

SATURDAY 15 / SUNDAY 16

Make a list of physical activities you either enjoy or *must* do, like dancing or mowing the lawn. When you feel the urge to eat, try something on your list. This way, you'll have fun, get things done, and feel better too!

WEEKLY FOOD DIARY

	MONDAY	TUESDAY	WEDNESDAY	THURSDAY	FRIDAY	SATURDAY	SUNDAY
DAILY TOTALS	MILK FAT PROTEIN VEG BREAD FRUIT	MILK FAT PROTEIN VEG BREAD FRUIT	MILK FAT PROTEIN VEG BREAD FRUIT	MILK FAT PROTEIN VEG BREAD FRUIT	MILK FAT PROTEIN VEG BREAD FRUIT	MILK FAT PROTEIN VEG BREAD FRUIT	MILK FAT PROTEIN VEG BREAD FRUIT
BREAKFAST							
LUNCH							
DINNER							
SNACKS							

FLOATER®

WEEKLY LIMITS EGGS/ORGAN MEAT _____ CHEESE/MEAT _____

OPTIONAL CALORIES _____

I will attend my Weight Watchers meeting this week on _____

MAY 1993

GOAL:

MONDAY 17

TUESDAY 18

WEDNESDAY 19

THURSDAY 20

FRIDAY 21

SATURDAY 22 / SUNDAY 23

When you eat properly and exercise regularly, you become a new person.
The meetings give me a lot of courage when I need it and help me to
go on.

—Diana Ferrara

WEEKLY FOOD DIARY

	MONDAY	TUESDAY	WEDNESDAY	THURSDAY	FRIDAY	SATURDAY	SUNDAY
TOTALS	MILK FAT PROTEIN VEG BREAD FRUIT	MILK FAT PROTEIN VEG BREAD FRUIT	MILK FAT PROTEIN VEG BREAD FRUIT	MILK FAT PROTEIN VEG BREAD FRUIT	MILK FAT PROTEIN VEG BREAD FRUIT	MILK FAT PROTEIN VEG BREAD FRUIT	MILK FAT PROTEIN VEG BREAD FRUIT
BREAKFAST							
LUNCH							
DINNER							
SNACKS							

WEEKLY LIMITS EGGS/ORGAN MEAT _____ CHEESE/MEAT _____

FLOATER®

OPTIONAL CALORIES

I will attend my Weight Watchers meeting this week on _____

MAY 1993

GOAL:

MONDAY 24

TUESDAY 25

WEDNESDAY 26

THURSDAY 27

FRIDAY 28

SATURDAY 29 / SUNDAY 30

Boredom can trigger between-meal eating—when you're not really hungry. Make a list of "boredom busters"—things you enjoy doing that are easy to start and stop.

JUNE 1993

SUNDAY	MONDAY	TUESDAY	WEDNESDAY
		1	2
6	7	8	9
13	14 FLAG DAY	15	16
20 FATHER'S DAY	21	22	23
27	28	29	30

JUNE 1993

THURSDAY	FRIDAY	SATURDAY	NOTES
3	4	5	
10	11	12	
17	18	19	
24	25	26	

WEEKLY FOOD DIARY

	MONDAY	TUESDAY	WEDNESDAY	THURSDAY	FRIDAY	SATURDAY	SUNDAY
DAILY TOTALS	MILK FAT PROTEIN VEG BREAD FRUIT	MILK FAT PROTEIN VEG BREAD FRUIT	MILK FAT PROTEIN VEG BREAD FRUIT	MILK FAT PROTEIN VEG BREAD FRUIT	MILK FAT PROTEIN VEG BREAD FRUIT	MILK FAT PROTEIN VEG BREAD FRUIT	MILK FAT PROTEIN VEG BREAD FRUIT
BREAKFAST							
LUNCH							
DINNER							
SNACKS							

WEEKLY LIMITS EGGS/ORGAN MEAT _____ CHEESE/MEAT _____

FLOATER®

OPTIONAL CALORIES

I will attend my Weight Watchers meeting this week on _____

MAY / JUNE 1993

WEIGHT WATCHERS

GOAL:

MONDAY 31/ MEMORIAL DAY

TUESDAY 1

WEDNESDAY 2

THURSDAY 3

FRIDAY 4

SATURDAY 5 / SUNDAY 6

Cleaning up after a meal can be a trigger for "extra" eating. Have someone else clean up, and stay out of the kitchen until leftovers are put away. You can also prepare less food to eliminate leftovers, have storage containers out, and have the sink filled with soapy water *before* you begin your meal.

WEEKLY FOOD DIARY

	MONDAY	TUESDAY	WEDNESDAY	THURSDAY	FRIDAY	SATURDAY	SUNDAY
DAILY TOTALS	MILK ___ FAT ___ PROTEIN ___ VEG ___ BREAD ___ FRUIT ___	MILK ___ FAT ___ PROTEIN ___ VEG ___ BREAD ___ FRUIT ___	MILK ___ FAT ___ PROTEIN ___ VEG ___ BREAD ___ FRUIT ___	MILK ___ FAT ___ PROTEIN ___ VEG ___ BREAD ___ FRUIT ___	MILK ___ FAT ___ PROTEIN ___ VEG ___ BREAD ___ FRUIT ___	MILK ___ FAT ___ PROTEIN ___ VEG ___ BREAD ___ FRUIT ___	MILK ___ FAT ___ PROTEIN ___ VEG ___ BREAD ___ FRUIT ___
BREAKFAST							
LUNCH							
DINNER							
SNACKS							

WEEKLY LIMITS EGGS/ORGAN MEAT _____ CHEESE/MEAT _____ FLOATER® _____

I will attend my Weight Watchers meeting this week on _____ OPTIONAL CALORIES _____

JUNE 1993

GOAL:

MONDAY 7

TUESDAY 8

WEDNESDAY 9

THURSDAY 10

FRIDAY 11

SATURDAY 12 / SUNDAY 13

Stress is a fact of life—and a trigger for problem eating. Identify what causes stress, then think about how you would change the situation, including small steps. Decide to be active and begin to take these steps, one at a time. Evaluate the results and, if necessary, plan your next steps.

WEEKLY FOOD DIARY

	MONDAY	TUESDAY	WEDNESDAY	THURSDAY	FRIDAY	SATURDAY	SUNDAY
DAILY TOTALS	MILK___ FAT___ PROTEIN___ VEG___ BREAD___ FRUIT___	MILK___ FAT___ PROTEIN___ VEG___ BREAD___ FRUIT___	MILK___ FAT___ PROTEIN___ VEG___ BREAD___ FRUIT___	MILK___ FAT___ PROTEIN___ VEG___ BREAD___ FRUIT___	MILK___ FAT___ PROTEIN___ VEG___ BREAD___ FRUIT___	MILK___ FAT___ PROTEIN___ VEG___ BREAD___ FRUIT___	MILK___ FAT___ PROTEIN___ VEG___ BREAD___ FRUIT___
BREAKFAST							
LUNCH							
DINNER							
SNACKS							

WEEKLY LIMITS EGGS/ORGAN MEAT _____ CHEESE/MEAT _____ FLOATER®

OPTIONAL CALORIES

I will attend my Weight Watchers meeting this week on _____

JUNE 1993

GOAL:

MONDAY 14 / FLAG DAY

TUESDAY 15

WEDNESDAY 16

THURSDAY 17

FRIDAY 18

SATURDAY 19 / SUNDAY 20 / FATHER'S DAY

When I eat out, I always order a salad with dressing on the side. I then dip my fork in the dressing before helping myself to salad. I get the taste of the dressing while actually using very little.

—*Susan Hickey*

WEEKLY FOOD DIARY

	MONDAY	TUESDAY	WEDNESDAY	THURSDAY	FRIDAY	SATURDAY	SUNDAY
DAILY TOTALS	MILK ___ FAT ___ PROTEIN ___ VEG ___ BREAD ___ FRUIT ___	MILK ___ FAT ___ PROTEIN ___ VEG ___ BREAD ___ FRUIT ___	MILK ___ FAT ___ PROTEIN ___ VEG ___ BREAD ___ FRUIT ___	MILK ___ FAT ___ PROTEIN ___ VEG ___ BREAD ___ FRUIT ___	MILK ___ FAT ___ PROTEIN ___ VEG ___ BREAD ___ FRUIT ___	MILK ___ FAT ___ PROTEIN ___ VEG ___ BREAD ___ FRUIT ___	MILK ___ FAT ___ PROTEIN ___ VEG ___ BREAD ___ FRUIT ___
BREAKFAST							
LUNCH							
DINNER							
SNACKS							

WEEKLY LIMITS EGGS/ORGAN MEAT ___ CHEESE/MEAT ___ FLOATER® ___ OPTIONAL CALORIES ___

I will attend my Weight Watchers meeting this week on ___

JUNE 1993

GOAL:

MONDAY 21

TUESDAY 22

WEDNESDAY 23

THURSDAY 24

FRIDAY 25

SATURDAY 26 / SUNDAY 27

If your stomach doesn't feel empty, chances are you're not hungry. And if something is eating at *you*, the urge to eat is in your mind.

JULY 1993

SUNDAY	MONDAY	TUESDAY	WEDNESDAY
4	5	6	7
INDEPENDENCE DAY			
11	12	13	14
18	19	20	21
25	26	27	28

JULY 1993

THURSDAY	FRIDAY	SATURDAY	NOTES
1	2	3	
8	9	10	
15	16	17	
22	23	24	
29	30	31	

WEEKLY FOOD DIARY

	MONDAY	TUESDAY	WEDNESDAY	THURSDAY	FRIDAY	SATURDAY	SUNDAY
DAILY TOTALS	MILK FAT PROTEIN VEG BREAD FRUIT	MILK FAT PROTEIN VEG BREAD FRUIT	MILK FAT PROTEIN VEG BREAD FRUIT	MILK FAT PROTEIN VEG BREAD FRUIT	MILK FAT PROTEIN VEG BREAD FRUIT	MILK FAT PROTEIN VEG BREAD FRUIT	MILK FAT PROTEIN VEG BREAD FRUIT
BREAKFAST							
LUNCH							
DINNER							
SNACKS							

WEEKLY LIMITS EGGS/ORGAN MEAT _____ CHEESE/MEAT _____ FLOATER® _____

OPTIONAL CALORIES _____

I will attend my Weight Watchers meeting this week on _____

JUNE / JULY 1993

GOAL:

MONDAY 28

TUESDAY 29

WEDNESDAY 30

THURSDAY 1

FRIDAY 2

SATURDAY 3 / SUNDAY 4 / INDEPENDENCE DAY

If you measure your weight-loss success only by pounds off at the scale, you may be headed for disappointment. Successful weight control comes from recognizing—and appreciating—each small change of habit along the way.

WEEKLY FOOD DIARY

	MONDAY	TUESDAY	WEDNESDAY	THURSDAY	FRIDAY	SATURDAY	SUNDAY
DAILY TOTALS	MILK ___ FAT ___ PROTEIN ___ VEG ___ BREAD ___ FRUIT ___	MILK ___ FAT ___ PROTEIN ___ VEG ___ BREAD ___ FRUIT ___	MILK ___ FAT ___ PROTEIN ___ VEG ___ BREAD ___ FRUIT ___	MILK ___ FAT ___ PROTEIN ___ VEG ___ BREAD ___ FRUIT ___	MILK ___ FAT ___ PROTEIN ___ VEG ___ BREAD ___ FRUIT ___	MILK ___ FAT ___ PROTEIN ___ VEG ___ BREAD ___ FRUIT ___	MILK ___ FAT ___ PROTEIN ___ VEG ___ BREAD ___ FRUIT ___
BREAKFAST							
LUNCH							
DINNER							
SNACKS							

WEEKLY LIMITS EGGS/ORGAN MEAT ___ CHEESE/MEAT ___

FLOATER™

OPTIONAL CALORIES

I will attend my Weight Watchers meeting this week on ___

JULY 1993

GOAL:

MONDAY 5

TUESDAY 6

WEDNESDAY 7

THURSDAY 8

FRIDAY 9

SATURDAY 10 / SUNDAY 11

Love yourself, set realistic goals, try to meet them, and come to peace with the foods that surround you.

—Barbara Berger

WEEKLY FOOD DIARY

	MONDAY	TUESDAY	WEDNESDAY	THURSDAY	FRIDAY	SATURDAY	SUNDAY
DAILY TOTALS	MILK ___ FAT ___ PROTEIN ___ VEG ___ BREAD ___ FRUIT ___	MILK ___ FAT ___ PROTEIN ___ VEG ___ BREAD ___ FRUIT ___	MILK ___ FAT ___ PROTEIN ___ VEG ___ BREAD ___ FRUIT ___	MILK ___ FAT ___ PROTEIN ___ VEG ___ BREAD ___ FRUIT ___	MILK ___ FAT ___ PROTEIN ___ VEG ___ BREAD ___ FRUIT ___	MILK ___ FAT ___ PROTEIN ___ VEG ___ BREAD ___ FRUIT ___	MILK ___ FAT ___ PROTEIN ___ VEG ___ BREAD ___ FRUIT ___
BREAKFAST							
LUNCH							
DINNER							
SNACKS							

WEEKLY LIMITS EGGS/ORGAN MEAT _____ CHEESE/MEAT _____ FLOATER®

OPTIONAL CALORIES

I will attend my Weight Watchers meeting this week on _____

JULY 1993

GOAL:

MONDAY 12

TUESDAY 13

WEDNESDAY 14

THURSDAY 15

FRIDAY 16

SATURDAY 17 / SUNDAY 18

Start on the success track by listing some habits you'd like to change.
Then, keep a record of each time you make a different choice.

WEEKLY FOOD DIARY

	MONDAY	TUESDAY	WEDNESDAY	THURSDAY	FRIDAY	SATURDAY	SUNDAY
DAILY TOTALS	MILK___ FAT___ PROTEIN___ VEG___ BREAD___ FRUIT___	MILK___ FAT___ PROTEIN___ VEG___ BREAD___ FRUIT___	MILK___ FAT___ PROTEIN___ VEG___ BREAD___ FRUIT___	MILK___ FAT___ PROTEIN___ VEG___ BREAD___ FRUIT___	MILK___ FAT___ PROTEIN___ VEG___ BREAD___ FRUIT___	MILK___ FAT___ PROTEIN___ VEG___ BREAD___ FRUIT___	MILK___ FAT___ PROTEIN___ VEG___ BREAD___ FRUIT___
BREAKFAST							
LUNCH							
DINNER							
SNACKS							

WEEKLY LIMITS EGGS/ORGAN MEAT _____ CHEESE/MEAT _____ FLOATER® _____

OPTIONAL CALORIES _____

I will attend my Weight Watchers meeting this week on _____

JULY 1993

GOAL:

MONDAY 19

TUESDAY 20

WEDNESDAY 21

THURSDAY 22

FRIDAY 23

SATURDAY 24 / SUNDAY 25

Negative moods, like boredom, anger, or unhappiness, can be triggers for overeating, but you can learn to cope with these feelings. Try muscle relaxation. When you feel tense, quickly tighten then relax different parts of your body.

WEEKLY FOOD DIARY

	MONDAY	TUESDAY	WEDNESDAY	THURSDAY	FRIDAY	SATURDAY	SUNDAY
DAILY TOTALS	MILK FAT PROTEIN VEG BREAD FRUIT	MILK FAT PROTEIN VEG BREAD FRUIT	MILK FAT PROTEIN VEG BREAD FRUIT	MILK FAT PROTEIN VEG BREAD FRUIT	MILK FAT PROTEIN VEG BREAD FRUIT	MILK FAT PROTEIN VEG BREAD FRUIT	MILK FAT PROTEIN VEG BREAD FRUIT
BREAKFAST							
LUNCH							
DINNER							
SNACKS							

WEEKLY LIMITS EGGS/ORGAN MEAT _____ CHEESE/MEAT _____ FLOATER® _____

OPTIONAL CALORIES

I will attend my Weight Watchers meeting this week on _____

JULY / AUGUST 1993

GOAL:

MONDAY 26

TUESDAY 27

WEDNESDAY 28

THURSDAY 29

FRIDAY 30

SATURDAY 31 / SUNDAY 1

Take your time; the weight didn't appear overnight!

—Anne O'Brien

AUGUST 1993

SUNDAY	MONDAY	TUESDAY	WEDNESDAY
1	2	3	4
8	9	10	11
15	16	17	18
22	23	24	25
29	30	31	

AUGUST 1993

THURSDAY	FRIDAY	SATURDAY	NOTES
5	6	7	
12	13	14	
19	20	21	
26	27	28	

WEEKLY FOOD DIARY

	MONDAY	TUESDAY	WEDNESDAY	THURSDAY	FRIDAY	SATURDAY	SUNDAY
TOTALLY	MILK ___ FAT ___ PROTEIN ___ VEG ___ BREAD ___ FRUIT ___	MILK ___ FAT ___ PROTEIN ___ VEG ___ BREAD ___ FRUIT ___	MILK ___ FAT ___ PROTEIN ___ VEG ___ BREAD ___ FRUIT ___	MILK ___ FAT ___ PROTEIN ___ VEG ___ BREAD ___ FRUIT ___	MILK ___ FAT ___ PROTEIN ___ VEG ___ BREAD ___ FRUIT ___	MILK ___ FAT ___ PROTEIN ___ VEG ___ BREAD ___ FRUIT ___	MILK ___ FAT ___ PROTEIN ___ VEG ___ BREAD ___ FRUIT ___
BREAKFAST							
LUNCH							
DINNER							
SNACKS							

WEEKLY LIMITS   EGGS/ORGAN MEAT _____   CHEESE/MEAT _____   FLOATER® _____

I will attend my Weight Watchers meeting this week on _____   OPTIONAL CALORIES _____

AUGUST 1993

GOAL:

MONDAY 2

TUESDAY 3

WEDNESDAY 4

THURSDAY 5

FRIDAY 6

SATURDAY 7 / SUNDAY 8

Overeating can be devastating to self-esteem. If you feel the urge, try distracting yourself for at least ten minutes. Give yourself the chance to settle down and think more clearly.

WEEKLY FOOD DIARY

	MONDAY	TUESDAY	WEDNESDAY	THURSDAY	FRIDAY	SATURDAY	SUNDAY
DAILY TOTALS	MILK FAT PROTEIN VEG BREAD FRUIT	MILK FAT PROTEIN VEG BREAD FRUIT	MILK FAT PROTEIN VEG BREAD FRUIT	MILK FAT PROTEIN VEG BREAD FRUIT	MILK FAT PROTEIN VEG BREAD FRUIT	MILK FAT PROTEIN VEG BREAD FRUIT	MILK FAT PROTEIN VEG BREAD FRUIT
BREAKFAST							
LUNCH							
DINNER							
SNACKS							

WEEKLY LIMITS EGGS/ORGAN MEAT _____ CHEESE/MEAT _____ FLOATER®

OPTIONAL CALORIES

I will attend my Weight Watchers meeting this week on _____

AUGUST 1993

GOAL:

MONDAY 9

TUESDAY 10

WEDNESDAY 11

THURSDAY 12

FRIDAY 13

SATURDAY 14 / SUNDAY 15

Weekends can be a challenge when you're trying to lose weight. First, identify "high risk" times, then develop strategies to deal with them. Remember, planning and being prepared put you in charge.

WEEKLY FOOD DIARY

	MONDAY	TUESDAY	WEDNESDAY	THURSDAY	FRIDAY	SATURDAY	SUNDAY
DAILY TOTALS	MILK FAT PROTEIN VEG BREAD FRUIT	MILK FAT PROTEIN VEG BREAD FRUIT	MILK FAT PROTEIN VEG BREAD FRUIT	MILK FAT PROTEIN VEG BREAD FRUIT	MILK FAT PROTEIN VEG BREAD FRUIT	MILK FAT PROTEIN VEG BREAD FRUIT	MILK FAT PROTEIN VEG BREAD FRUIT
BREAKFAST							
LUNCH							
DINNER							
SNACKS							

WEEKLY LIMITS EGGS/ORGAN MEAT _____ CHEESE/MEAT _____ FLOATER® _____

OPTIONAL CALORIES

I will attend my Weight Watchers meeting this week on _____

AUGUST 1993

GOAL:

MONDAY 16

TUESDAY 17

WEDNESDAY 18

THURSDAY 19

FRIDAY 20

SATURDAY 21 / SUNDAY 22

Keep your perspective. You're sticking to your plan and eating healthier than ever before. Always keep in mind the weight you've already lost, which proves the process works.

WEEKLY FOOD DIARY

	MONDAY	TUESDAY	WEDNESDAY	THURSDAY	FRIDAY	SATURDAY	SUNDAY
DAILY TOTALS	MILK____ FAT____ PROTEIN____ VEG____ BREAD____ FRUIT____	MILK____ FAT____ PROTEIN____ VEG____ BREAD____ FRUIT____	MILK____ FAT____ PROTEIN____ VEG____ BREAD____ FRUIT____	MILK____ FAT____ PROTEIN____ VEG____ BREAD____ FRUIT____	MILK____ FAT____ PROTEIN____ VEG____ BREAD____ FRUIT____	MILK____ FAT____ PROTEIN____ VEG____ BREAD____ FRUIT____	MILK____ FAT____ PROTEIN____ VEG____ BREAD____ FRUIT____
BREAKFAST							
LUNCH							
DINNER							
SNACKS							

WEEKLY LIMITS EGGS/ORGAN MEAT _____ CHEESE/MEAT _____ FLOATER® _____

OPTIONAL CALORIES _____

I will attend my Weight Watchers meeting this week on _____

AUGUST 1993

GOAL:

MONDAY 23

TUESDAY 24

WEDNESDAY 25

THURSDAY 26

FRIDAY 27

SATURDAY 28 / SUNDAY 29

Praise yourself when you've done well and realize that if you slip up, you have the power to make it a temporary slip.

—Gail Corley

SEPTEMBER 1993

SUNDAY	MONDAY	TUESDAY	WEDNESDAY
			1
5	6 LABOR DAY	7	8
12	13	14	15
19	20	21	22
26	27	28	29

SEPTEMBER 1993

THURSDAY	FRIDAY	SATURDAY	NOTES
2	3	4	
9	10	11	
16 FIRST DAY OF ROSH HASHANAH	17	18	
23	24	25 YOM KIPPUR	
30			

WEEKLY FOOD DIARY

	MONDAY	TUESDAY	WEDNESDAY	THURSDAY	FRIDAY	SATURDAY	SUNDAY
DAILY TOTALS	MILK___ FAT___ PROTEIN___ VEG___ BREAD___ FRUIT___	MILK___ FAT___ PROTEIN___ VEG___ BREAD___ FRUIT___	MILK___ FAT___ PROTEIN___ VEG___ BREAD___ FRUIT___	MILK___ FAT___ PROTEIN___ VEG___ BREAD___ FRUIT___	MILK___ FAT___ PROTEIN___ VEG___ BREAD___ FRUIT___	MILK___ FAT___ PROTEIN___ VEG___ BREAD___ FRUIT___	MILK___ FAT___ PROTEIN___ VEG___ BREAD___ FRUIT___
BREAKFAST							
LUNCH							
DINNER							
SNACKS							

WEEKLY LIMITS EGGS/ORGAN MEAT _____ CHEESE/MEAT _____ FLOATER® _____

I will attend my Weight Watchers meeting this week on _____

OPTIONAL CALORIES

AUGUST / SEPTEMBER 1993

WEIGHT WATCHERS

GOAL:

MONDAY 30

TUESDAY 31

WEDNESDAY 1

THURSDAY 2

FRIDAY 3

SATURDAY 4 / SUNDAY 5

I give myself credit for every positive change I make in my eating behaviors, but I don't beat myself up when I regress.

—Virginia Miele

WEEKLY FOOD DIARY

	MONDAY	TUESDAY	WEDNESDAY	THURSDAY	FRIDAY	SATURDAY	SUNDAY
DAILY TOTALS	MILK ___ FAT ___ PROTEIN ___ VEG ___ BREAD ___ FRUIT ___	MILK ___ FAT ___ PROTEIN ___ VEG ___ BREAD ___ FRUIT ___	MILK ___ FAT ___ PROTEIN ___ VEG ___ BREAD ___ FRUIT ___	MILK ___ FAT ___ PROTEIN ___ VEG ___ BREAD ___ FRUIT ___	MILK ___ FAT ___ PROTEIN ___ VEG ___ BREAD ___ FRUIT ___	MILK ___ FAT ___ PROTEIN ___ VEG ___ BREAD ___ FRUIT ___	MILK ___ FAT ___ PROTEIN ___ VEG ___ BREAD ___ FRUIT ___
BREAKFAST							
LUNCH							
DINNER							
SNACKS							

WEEKLY LIMITS EGGS/ORGAN MEAT _____ CHEESE/MEAT _____ FLOATER® _____

OPTIONAL CALORIES _____

I will attend my Weight Watchers meeting this week on _____

SEPTEMBER 1993

GOAL :

MONDAY 6 / LABOR DAY

TUESDAY 7

WEDNESDAY 8

THURSDAY 9

FRIDAY 10

SATURDAY 11 / SUNDAY 12

When eating alone, treat yourself like company and set a nice table. Plan your meals carefully, with foods you really enjoy. Listen to relaxing music while you eat.

WEEKLY FOOD DIARY

	MONDAY	TUESDAY	WEDNESDAY	THURSDAY	FRIDAY	SATURDAY	SUNDAY
DAILY TOTALS	MILK ____ FAT ____ PROTEIN ____ VEG ____ BREAD ____ FRUIT ____	MILK ____ FAT ____ PROTEIN ____ VEG ____ BREAD ____ FRUIT ____	MILK ____ FAT ____ PROTEIN ____ VEG ____ BREAD ____ FRUIT ____	MILK ____ FAT ____ PROTEIN ____ VEG ____ BREAD ____ FRUIT ____	MILK ____ FAT ____ PROTEIN ____ VEG ____ BREAD ____ FRUIT ____	MILK ____ FAT ____ PROTEIN ____ VEG ____ BREAD ____ FRUIT ____	MILK ____ FAT ____ PROTEIN ____ VEG ____ BREAD ____ FRUIT ____
BREAKFAST							
LUNCH							
DINNER							
SNACKS							

WEEKLY LIMITS EGGS/ORGAN MEAT _____ CHEESE/MEAT _____

FLOATER®

OPTIONAL CALORIES

I will attend my Weight Watchers meeting this week on _____

SEPTEMBER 1993

WEIGHT WATCHERS

GOAL:

MONDAY 13

TUESDAY 14

WEDNESDAY 15

THURSDAY 16 / FIRST DAY OF ROSH HASHANAH

FRIDAY 17

SATURDAY 18 / SUNDAY 19

You know it takes many steps to reach a destination. It takes each small achievement to reach your weight-loss goal. Focus on the little accomplishments—because each small step takes you that much closer to your goal.

WEEKLY FOOD DIARY

	MONDAY	TUESDAY	WEDNESDAY	THURSDAY	FRIDAY	SATURDAY	SUNDAY
DAILY TOTALS	MILK FAT PROTEIN VEG BREAD FRUIT	MILK FAT PROTEIN VEG BREAD FRUIT	MILK FAT PROTEIN VEG BREAD FRUIT	MILK FAT PROTEIN VEG BREAD FRUIT	MILK FAT PROTEIN VEG BREAD FRUIT	MILK FAT PROTEIN VEG BREAD FRUIT	MILK FAT PROTEIN VEG BREAD FRUIT
BREAKFAST							
LUNCH							
DINNER							
SNACKS							

WEEKLY LIMITS EGGS/ORGAN MEAT _____ CHEESE/MEAT _____ FLOATER® _____

OPTIONAL CALORIES

I will attend my Weight Watchers meeting this week on

SEPTEMBER 1993

GOAL:

MONDAY 20

TUESDAY 21

WEDNESDAY 22

THURSDAY 23

FRIDAY 24

SATURDAY 25 / YOM KIPPUR / SUNDAY 26

I have learned to eat normally to feed my body, not in emotional binges. It feels wonderful to have control without deprivation.

—Wendy Pacelli

OCTOBER 1993

SUNDAY	MONDAY	TUESDAY	WEDNESDAY
3	4	5	6
10	11 COLUMBUS DAY	12	13
17	18	19	20
24	25	26	27
31 HALLOWEEN DST ENDS			

OCTOBER 1993

THURSDAY	FRIDAY	SATURDAY	NOTES
	1	2	
7	8	9	
14	15	16	
21	22	23	
28	29	30	

WEEKLY FOOD DIARY

	MONDAY	TUESDAY	WEDNESDAY	THURSDAY	FRIDAY	SATURDAY	SUNDAY
DAILY TOTALS	MILK FAT PROTEIN VEG BREAD FRUIT	MILK FAT PROTEIN VEG BREAD FRUIT	MILK FAT PROTEIN VEG BREAD FRUIT	MILK FAT PROTEIN VEG BREAD FRUIT	MILK FAT PROTEIN VEG BREAD FRUIT	MILK FAT PROTEIN VEG BREAD FRUIT	MILK FAT PROTEIN VEG BREAD FRUIT
BREAKFAST							
LUNCH							
DINNER							
SNACKS							

WEEKLY LIMITS   EGGS/ORGAN MEAT _____   CHEESE/MEAT _____   FLOATER™ _____

I will attend my Weight Watchers meeting this week on _____   OPTIONAL CALORIES _____

SEPTEMBER / OCTOBER 1993

GOAL:

MONDAY 27

TUESDAY 28

WEDNESDAY 29

THURSDAY 30

FRIDAY 1

SATURDAY 2 / SUNDAY 3

Kitchen tip: Refrigerate soups and stews overnight and skim off fat the next day.

W E E K L Y   F O O D   D I A R Y

	MONDAY	TUESDAY	WEDNESDAY	THURSDAY	FRIDAY	SATURDAY	SUNDAY
DAILY TOTALS	MILK FAT PROTEIN VEG BREAD FRUIT	MILK FAT PROTEIN VEG BREAD FRUIT	MILK FAT PROTEIN VEG BREAD FRUIT	MILK FAT PROTEIN VEG BREAD FRUIT	MILK FAT PROTEIN VEG BREAD FRUIT	MILK FAT PROTEIN VEG BREAD FRUIT	MILK FAT PROTEIN VEG BREAD FRUIT
BREAKFAST							
LUNCH							
DINNER							
SNACKS							

WEEKLY LIMITS EGGS/ORGAN MEAT _____ CHEESE/MEAT _____ FLOATER®

I will attend my Weight Watchers meeting this week on _____ OPTIONAL CALORIES

OCTOBER 1993

GOAL:

MONDAY 4

TUESDAY 5

WEDNESDAY 6

THURSDAY 7

FRIDAY 8

SATURDAY 9 / SUNDAY 10

Problem eating can happen between dinner and bedtime, when you're tired and time is less structured. If you feel like eating, have a planned snack if you're really hungry. But if you're not hungry, skip the snack and take a warm bath or try a little exercise.

WEEKLY FOOD DIARY

	MONDAY	TUESDAY	WEDNESDAY	THURSDAY	FRIDAY	SATURDAY	SUNDAY
DAILY TOTALS	MILK____ FAT____ PROTEIN____ VEG____ BREAD____ FRUIT____	MILK____ FAT____ PROTEIN____ VEG____ BREAD____ FRUIT____	MILK____ FAT____ PROTEIN____ VEG____ BREAD____ FRUIT____	MILK____ FAT____ PROTEIN____ VEG____ BREAD____ FRUIT____	MILK____ FAT____ PROTEIN____ VEG____ BREAD____ FRUIT____	MILK____ FAT____ PROTEIN____ VEG____ BREAD____ FRUIT____	MILK____ FAT____ PROTEIN____ VEG____ BREAD____ FRUIT____
BREAKFAST							
LUNCH							
DINNER							
SNACKS							

WEEKLY LIMITS EGGS/ORGAN MEAT _____ CHEESE/MEAT _____ FLOATER® _____

OPTIONAL CALORIES _____

I will attend my Weight Watchers meeting this week on _____

OCTOBER 1993

GOAL:

MONDAY 11 / COLUMBUS DAY

TUESDAY 12

WEDNESDAY 13

THURSDAY 14

FRIDAY 15

SATURDAY 16 / SUNDAY 17

A new outfit, a manicure, or a bubble bath helps replace my old habit of food as a reward. Not waiting to enjoy things when I'm thin has reduced my stress and, I believe, made my weight loss easier.

—Regina Walker

WEEKLY FOOD DIARY

	MONDAY	TUESDAY	WEDNESDAY	THURSDAY	FRIDAY	SATURDAY	SUNDAY
DAILY TOTALS	MILK ___ FAT ___ PROTEIN ___ VEG ___ BREAD ___ FRUIT ___	MILK ___ FAT ___ PROTEIN ___ VEG ___ BREAD ___ FRUIT ___	MILK ___ FAT ___ PROTEIN ___ VEG ___ BREAD ___ FRUIT ___	MILK ___ FAT ___ PROTEIN ___ VEG ___ BREAD ___ FRUIT ___	MILK ___ FAT ___ PROTEIN ___ VEG ___ BREAD ___ FRUIT ___	MILK ___ FAT ___ PROTEIN ___ VEG ___ BREAD ___ FRUIT ___	MILK ___ FAT ___ PROTEIN ___ VEG ___ BREAD ___ FRUIT ___
BREAKFAST							
LUNCH							
DINNER							
SNACKS							

WEEKLY LIMITS EGGS/ORGAN MEAT _____ CHEESE/MEAT _____ FLOATER℠ _____

OPTIONAL CALORIES _____

I will attend my Weight Watchers meeting this week on _____

OCTOBER 1993

GOAL:

MONDAY 18

TUESDAY 19

WEDNESDAY 20

THURSDAY 21

FRIDAY 22

SATURDAY 23 / SUNDAY 24

When invited to a cocktail party, eat before you go. Once you're there, sip a light drink and enjoy the party!

W E E K L Y   F O O D   D I A R Y

	MONDAY	TUESDAY	WEDNESDAY	THURSDAY	FRIDAY	SATURDAY	SUNDAY
DAILY TOTALS	MILK ___ FAT ___ PROTEIN ___ VEG ___ BREAD ___ FRUIT ___	MILK ___ FAT ___ PROTEIN ___ VEG ___ BREAD ___ FRUIT ___	MILK ___ FAT ___ PROTEIN ___ VEG ___ BREAD ___ FRUIT ___	MILK ___ FAT ___ PROTEIN ___ VEG ___ BREAD ___ FRUIT ___	MILK ___ FAT ___ PROTEIN ___ VEG ___ BREAD ___ FRUIT ___	MILK ___ FAT ___ PROTEIN ___ VEG ___ BREAD ___ FRUIT ___	MILK ___ FAT ___ PROTEIN ___ VEG ___ BREAD ___ FRUIT ___
BREAKFAST							
LUNCH							
DINNER							
SNACKS							

WEEKLY LIMITS EGGS/ORGAN MEAT _____ CHEESE/MEAT _____ FLOATER® _____

I will attend my Weight Watchers meeting this week on _____ OPTIONAL CALORIES _____

OCTOBER 1993

GOAL:

MONDAY 25

TUESDAY 26

WEDNESDAY 27

THURSDAY 28

FRIDAY 29

SATURDAY 30 / SUNDAY 31 / HALLOWEEN / DST ENDS

As a late-night treat, I make a shake of skim milk and fruit; it's cold, frothy, and healthy and a relaxing way to end a hectic day.

—Gloria J. Danet

NOVEMBER 1993

SUNDAY	MONDAY	TUESDAY	WEDNESDAY
	1	2 ELECTION DAY	3
7	8	9	10
14	15	16	17
21	22	23	24
28	29	30	

NOVEMBER 1993

THURSDAY	FRIDAY	SATURDAY	NOTES
4	5	6	
11 VETERANS DAY	12	13	
18	19	20	
25 THANKSGIVING	26	27	

WEEKLY FOOD DIARY

	MONDAY	TUESDAY	WEDNESDAY	THURSDAY	FRIDAY	SATURDAY	SUNDAY
	MILK FAT PROTEIN VEG BREAD FRUIT	MILK FAT PROTEIN VEG BREAD FRUIT	MILK FAT PROTEIN VEG BREAD FRUIT	MILK FAT PROTEIN VEG BREAD FRUIT	MILK FAT PROTEIN VEG BREAD FRUIT	MILK FAT PROTEIN VEG BREAD FRUIT	MILK FAT PROTEIN VEG BREAD FRUIT
DAILY TOTALS							
BREAKFAST							
LUNCH							
DINNER							
SNACKS							

WEEKLY LIMITS EGGS/ORGAN MEAT _____ CHEESE/MEAT _____ FLOATER®

OPTIONAL CALORIES

I will attend my Weight Watchers meeting this week on _____

NOVEMBER 1993

GOAL:

MONDAY 1

TUESDAY 2 / ELECTION DAY

WEDNESDAY 3

THURSDAY 4

FRIDAY 5

SATURDAY 6 / SUNDAY 7

When you've decided to lose weight, always keep in mind why—for your health or to be more attractive, or simply because you know you'll feel better. Whatever your reason, keeping it in mind at all times will help you through difficult moments. Be sure to make realistic goals for yourself.

WEEKLY FOOD DIARY

	MONDAY	TUESDAY	WEDNESDAY	THURSDAY	FRIDAY	SATURDAY	SUNDAY
DAILY TOTALS	MILK ___ FAT ___ PROTEIN ___ VEG ___ BREAD ___ FRUIT ___	MILK ___ FAT ___ PROTEIN ___ VEG ___ BREAD ___ FRUIT ___	MILK ___ FAT ___ PROTEIN ___ VEG ___ BREAD ___ FRUIT ___	MILK ___ FAT ___ PROTEIN ___ VEG ___ BREAD ___ FRUIT ___	MILK ___ FAT ___ PROTEIN ___ VEG ___ BREAD ___ FRUIT ___	MILK ___ FAT ___ PROTEIN ___ VEG ___ BREAD ___ FRUIT ___	MILK ___ FAT ___ PROTEIN ___ VEG ___ BREAD ___ FRUIT ___
BREAKFAST							
LUNCH							
DINNER							
SNACKS							

WEEKLY LIMITS EGGS/ORGAN MEAT _____ CHEESE/MEAT _____ FLOATER® _____

I will attend my Weight Watchers meeting this week on _____

OPTIONAL CALORIES

NOVEMBER 1993

GOAL:

MONDAY 8

TUESDAY 9

WEDNESDAY 10

THURSDAY 11 / VETERANS DAY

FRIDAY 12

SATURDAY 13 / SUNDAY 14

When you eat alone, you may tend to eat quickly, with less fuss, less planning, and less enjoyment. Turn this around and make it a fun, relaxing time.

WEEKLY FOOD DIARY

	MONDAY	TUESDAY	WEDNESDAY	THURSDAY	FRIDAY	SATURDAY	SUNDAY
DAILY TOTALS	MILK FAT PROTEIN VEG BREAD FRUIT	MILK FAT PROTEIN VEG BREAD FRUIT	MILK FAT PROTEIN VEG BREAD FRUIT	MILK FAT PROTEIN VEG BREAD FRUIT	MILK FAT PROTEIN VEG BREAD FRUIT	MILK FAT PROTEIN VEG BREAD FRUIT	MILK FAT PROTEIN VEG BREAD FRUIT
BREAKFAST							
LUNCH							
DINNER							
SNACKS							

WEEKLY LIMITS EGGS/ORGAN MEAT _____ CHEESE/MEAT _____ FLOATER℠ _____

OPTIONAL CALORIES _____

I will attend my Weight Watchers meeting this week on _____

NOVEMBER 1993

GOAL:

MONDAY 15

TUESDAY 16

WEDNESDAY 17

THURSDAY 18

FRIDAY 19

SATURDAY 20 / SUNDAY 21

Kitchen tip: Cut all the visible fat from meats and skin from poultry before cooking.

WEEKLY FOOD DIARY

	MONDAY	TUESDAY	WEDNESDAY	THURSDAY	FRIDAY	SATURDAY	SUNDAY
DAILY TOTALS	MILK FAT PROTEIN VEG BREAD FRUIT	MILK FAT PROTEIN VEG BREAD FRUIT	MILK FAT PROTEIN VEG BREAD FRUIT	MILK FAT PROTEIN VEG BREAD FRUIT	MILK FAT PROTEIN VEG BREAD FRUIT	MILK FAT PROTEIN VEG BREAD FRUIT	MILK FAT PROTEIN VEG BREAD FRUIT
BREAKFAST							
LUNCH							
DINNER							
SNACKS							

FLOATER®

OPTIONAL CALORIES

WEEKLY LIMITS EGGS/ORGAN MEAT _____ CHEESE/MEAT _____

I will attend my Weight Watchers meeting this week on _____

NOVEMBER 1993

GOAL:

MONDAY 22

TUESDAY 23

WEDNESDAY 24

THURSDAY 25 / THANKSGIVING

FRIDAY 26

SATURDAY 27 / SUNDAY 28

I try not to deny myself a desired food but postpone having it for an hour or two . . . sometimes three. Usually the craving passes and I am able to stay on my food plan.

—*Bernadette Hayes-Griffin*

DECEMBER 1993

SUNDAY	MONDAY	TUESDAY	WEDNESDAY
			1
5	6	7	8
12	13	14	15
19	20	21	22
26	27	28	29

DECEMBER 1993

THURSDAY	FRIDAY	SATURDAY	NOTES
2	3	4	
9 FIRST DAY OF HANUKKAH	10	11	
16	17	18	
23	24	25 CHRISTMAS	
30	31		

WEEKLY FOOD DIARY

	MONDAY	TUESDAY	WEDNESDAY	THURSDAY	FRIDAY	SATURDAY	SUNDAY
TOTALS	MILK FAT PROTEIN VEG BREAD FRUIT	MILK FAT PROTEIN VEG BREAD FRUIT	MILK FAT PROTEIN VEG BREAD FRUIT	MILK FAT PROTEIN VEG BREAD FRUIT	MILK FAT PROTEIN VEG BREAD FRUIT	MILK FAT PROTEIN VEG BREAD FRUIT	MILK FAT PROTEIN VEG BREAD FRUIT
BREAKFAST							
LUNCH							
DINNER							
SNACKS							

WEEKLY LIMITS EGGS/ORGAN MEAT _____ CHEESE/MEAT _____ FLOATER®_____

OPTIONAL CALORIES _____

I will attend my Weight Watchers meeting this week on _____

NOVEMBER / DECEMBER 1993

GOAL:

MONDAY 29

TUESDAY 30

WEDNESDAY 1

THURSDAY 2

FRIDAY 3

SATURDAY 4 / SUNDAY 5

To keep on top of your resolution to exercise, be sure to make it fun—
something you'll look forward to. Choose activities and surroundings that
you enjoy. For example, walk outdoors with a friend or use a stationary
bike indoors while watching your favorite television show.

WEEKLY FOOD DIARY

	MONDAY	TUESDAY	WEDNESDAY	THURSDAY	FRIDAY	SATURDAY	SUNDAY
DAILY TOTALS	MILK FAT PROTEIN VEG BREAD FRUIT	MILK FAT PROTEIN VEG BREAD FRUIT	MILK FAT PROTEIN VEG BREAD FRUIT	MILK FAT PROTEIN VEG BREAD FRUIT	MILK FAT PROTEIN VEG BREAD FRUIT	MILK FAT PROTEIN VEG BREAD FRUIT	MILK FAT PROTEIN VEG BREAD FRUIT
BREAKFAST							
LUNCH							
DINNER							
SNACKS							

WEEKLY LIMITS   EGGS/ORGAN MEAT _____   CHEESE/MEAT _____

FLOATER®

I will attend my Weight Watchers meeting this week on _____

OPTIONAL CALORIES

DECEMBER 1993

GOAL:

MONDAY 6

TUESDAY 7

WEDNESDAY 8

THURSDAY 9 / FIRST DAY OF HANUKKAH

FRIDAY 10

SATURDAY 11 / SUNDAY 12

Hunger is *physiological*—a need to eat caused by lack of food. Appetite is a *psychological* interest in food or drink. You can control your weight by learning to eat only when you're really hungry.

WEEKLY FOOD DIARY

	MONDAY	TUESDAY	WEDNESDAY	THURSDAY	FRIDAY	SATURDAY	SUNDAY
DAILY TOTALS	MILK ___ FAT ___ PROTEIN ___ VEG ___ BREAD ___ FRUIT ___	MILK ___ FAT ___ PROTEIN ___ VEG ___ BREAD ___ FRUIT ___	MILK ___ FAT ___ PROTEIN ___ VEG ___ BREAD ___ FRUIT ___	MILK ___ FAT ___ PROTEIN ___ VEG ___ BREAD ___ FRUIT ___	MILK ___ FAT ___ PROTEIN ___ VEG ___ BREAD ___ FRUIT ___	MILK ___ FAT ___ PROTEIN ___ VEG ___ BREAD ___ FRUIT ___	MILK ___ FAT ___ PROTEIN ___ VEG ___ BREAD ___ FRUIT ___
BREAKFAST							
LUNCH							
DINNER							
SNACKS							

WEEKLY LIMITS EGGS/ORGAN MEAT ___ CHEESE/MEAT ___

FLOATER®

I will attend my Weight Watchers meeting this week on ___

OPTIONAL CALORIES

DECEMBER 1993

WEIGHT WATCHERS

GOAL:

MONDAY 13

TUESDAY 14

WEDNESDAY 15

THURSDAY 16

FRIDAY 17

SATURDAY 18 / SUNDAY 19

Kitchen tip: For an almost fat-free gravy, thicken broth or bouillon with cornstarch.

W E E K L Y   F O O D   D I A R Y

	MONDAY	TUESDAY	WEDNESDAY	THURSDAY	FRIDAY	SATURDAY	SUNDAY
DAILY TOTALS	MILK ___ FAT ___ PROTEIN ___ VEG ___ BREAD ___ FRUIT ___	MILK ___ FAT ___ PROTEIN ___ VEG ___ BREAD ___ FRUIT ___	MILK ___ FAT ___ PROTEIN ___ VEG ___ BREAD ___ FRUIT ___	MILK ___ FAT ___ PROTEIN ___ VEG ___ BREAD ___ FRUIT ___	MILK ___ FAT ___ PROTEIN ___ VEG ___ BREAD ___ FRUIT ___	MILK ___ FAT ___ PROTEIN ___ VEG ___ BREAD ___ FRUIT ___	MILK ___ FAT ___ PROTEIN ___ VEG ___ BREAD ___ FRUIT ___
BREAKFAST							
LUNCH							
DINNER							
SNACKS							

WEEKLY LIMITS EGGS/ORGAN MEAT _____ CHEESE/MEAT _____ FLOATER® _____

I will attend my Weight Watchers meeting this week on _____ OPTIONAL CALORIES _____

DECEMBER 1993

WEIGHT WATCHERS

GOAL:

MONDAY 20

TUESDAY 21

WEDNESDAY 22

THURSDAY 23

FRIDAY 24

SATURDAY 25 / CHRISTMAS / SUNDAY 26

Focus on foods that you like and work them into your menus. Choose an exercise that's fun and do it regularly; it helps weight loss and relieves tension. If you lapse, don't feel guilty but go right back to the food plan.

—*Edith L. Adams-Foose*

WEEKLY FOOD DIARY

	MONDAY	TUESDAY	WEDNESDAY	THURSDAY	FRIDAY	SATURDAY	SUNDAY
DAILY TOTALS	MILK___ FAT___ PROTEIN___ VEG___ BREAD___ FRUIT___	MILK___ FAT___ PROTEIN___ VEG___ BREAD___ FRUIT___	MILK___ FAT___ PROTEIN___ VEG___ BREAD___ FRUIT___	MILK___ FAT___ PROTEIN___ VEG___ BREAD___ FRUIT___	MILK___ FAT___ PROTEIN___ VEG___ BREAD___ FRUIT___	MILK___ FAT___ PROTEIN___ VEG___ BREAD___ FRUIT___	MILK___ FAT___ PROTEIN___ VEG___ BREAD___ FRUIT___
BREAKFAST							
LUNCH							
DINNER							
SNACKS							

WEEKLY LIMITS EGGS/ORGAN MEAT _____ CHEESE/MEAT _____ FLOATER®

I will attend my Weight Watchers meeting this week on _____ OPTIONAL CALORIES

DECEMBER / JANUARY 1993–94

GOAL :

MONDAY 27

TUESDAY 28

WEDNESDAY 29

THURSDAY 30

FRIDAY 31

SATURDAY 1 / NEW YEAR'S DAY / SUNDAY 2

If you've decided to lose weight, an important way to stay motivated is to rely on measures other than the scale. For example, measure your success by how your clothes fit and how much better you feel.

RECIPES

Cream of Mushroom Soup

Microwave Cream of Tomato Soup with Rice

Vegetable Noodle Soup

Hot Open-Faced Turkey Sandwich with Gravy

Peanut Butter–Banana Sandwich

Pizza Muffins

Macaroni and Cheese

Eggplant Parmigiana

Lasagna

Spicy Hamburger Pie

Fish Cakes

Fisherman's Pie

Lemon Chicken

Savory Chicken Loaf

Veal Stew with Dumplings

Kasha Stuffed Peppers

Glazed Butternut Squash

Barbecued Corn on the Cob

Vegetables Au Gratin

Cole Slaw

Individual Cherry Cobblers

Meringue-Capped Rice Pudding

Microwave Fruit Compote

Spice Muffins with Maple Icing

Strawberry Meringue Tarts with Chocolate Syrup

Apple Crumb Pie

UNDERSTANDING
THE RECIPES

To help you keep track of your choices on the Food Plan, we've provided the Selection™ Information for each recipe. You'll see, for example, that one serving of a recipe provides 1 Milk, 2 Proteins, and 15 Optional Calories. (Be sure to recalculate the Selection Information if you make any changes to a recipe.)

Each recipe also includes a per-serving nutritional analysis of calories, protein, fat, carbohydrate, calcium, sodium, cholesterol, and dietary fiber. These figures are for the recipe *exactly as shown*. For example, the nutritional analyses for recipes containing cooked items such as rice, pasta, or vegetables assume that no extra salt or fat will be added during cooking. If you decide to add salt or fat, you alter the nutritional information shown for the recipe—whether or not the changes affect the Selection Information.

Many recipes are reduced in sodium or cholesterol, or have 30 percent or less calories from fat. Oftentimes we've used egg substitutes, reduced-fat cheeses, and low-sodium broths in recipes with excellent results:

- "Reduced cholesterol" means that a dish containing 2 or more Proteins has 50 milligrams or less of cholesterol per serving. All other recipes so noted contain 25 milligrams or less of cholesterol per serving.
- "Reduced fat" indicates that 30 percent or less of the calories come from fat.
- "Reduced sodium" means that a dish containing 2 or more Proteins has 400 milligrams or less of sodium per serving. All other recipes so noted contain 200 milligrams or less of sodium per serving.

A NOTE ABOUT
MICROWAVE RECIPES

All microwave recipes were tested in 650- to 700-watt microwave ovens.

Cream of Mushroom Soup

PREP TIME: 5 MINUTES
COOKING TIME: 25 MINUTES
TOTAL TIME: 30 MINUTES

1 tablespoon plus 1 teaspoon olive oil	2 cups canned chicken broth
½ cup diced onion	1 cup lowfat milk (2% milkfat)
1 clove garlic, minced	
1½ cups sliced mushrooms	1 tablespoon minced fresh parsley
2 tablespoons all-purpose flour	Dash salt and pepper

1. In a 2-quart saucepan heat oil; add onion and garlic and cook over medium-high heat until onion is tender, about 2 minutes.
2. Add mushrooms and cook, stirring occasionally, for 2 minutes. Sprinkle in flour and stir until combined, about 1 minute.
3. Add remaining ingredients; reduce heat and simmer for 20 minutes, stirring frequently.

MAKES 4 SERVINGS, ABOUT 1 CUP EACH

Each serving provides: ¼ Milk; 1 Fat; 1 Vegetable; 43 Optional Calories.

Per serving: 113 calories; 5 g protein; 7 g fat; 9 g carbohydrate; 89 mg calcium; 559 mg sodium; 5 mg cholesterol; 1 g dietary fiber

Reduced cholesterol

Microwave Cream of Tomato Soup with Rice

PREP TIME: 5 MINUTES
COOKING TIME: 23 MINUTES
TOTAL TIME: 28 MINUTES

½ cup finely chopped shallots or onions
2 teaspoons vegetable oil
1½ cups canned Italian plum tomatoes, seeded (reserve liquid)
1 cup tomato juice
¼ cup dry white wine
2 ounces uncooked medium-grain rice

1 packet instant beef or chicken broth and seasoning mix
1 cup skim milk
¼ cup half-and-half
Dash salt and pepper
1 tablespoon chopped fresh Italian parsley or fresh basil

1. Combine shallots and oil in a 3-quart microwavable casserole; cover and microwave on High (100%) for 1½ minutes.

2. Place tomatoes in blender; process until pureed, about 30 seconds. Add tomatoes, reserved liquid, tomato juice, wine, rice, broth mix, and *1 cup water* to shallots. Microwave, covered, on High (100%) for 5 minutes, or until boiling. Microwave on Medium/High (70%) for 15 minutes, stirring every 5 minutes.

3. Gradually add milk and half-and-half to tomato mixture, stirring constantly. Cover and microwave on Low (30%) for 3 minutes, just until heated through. Season with salt and pepper and sprinkle with parsley.

MAKES 4 SERVINGS, ABOUT 1 CUP EACH

Each serving provides: ¼ Milk; ½ Fat; 1¼ Vegetables; ½ Bread; 40 Optional Calories.

Per serving: 168 calories; 6 g protein; 4 g fat; 25 g carbohydrate; 134 mg calcium; 675 mg sodium; 7 mg cholesterol; 1 g dietary fiber

Reduced cholesterol and fat

Vegetable Noodle Soup

PREP TIME: 5 MINUTES
COOKING TIME: 14 MINUTES
TOTAL TIME: 19 MINUTES

2 teaspoons vegetable oil	1½ ounces alphabet noodles
½ cup chopped onion	1 tablespoon all-purpose flour
½ cup chopped celery	1 tablespoon minced fresh parsley
½ cup diced carrot	Dash salt and pepper
½ cup sliced green beans	
½ cup torn spinach leaves	
1 garlic clove	
3 packets instant chicken broth and seasoning mix	

1. In a 4-quart microwavable casserole combine oil, vegetables, and garlic; stir to thoroughly coat vegetables. Cover with vented plastic wrap and microwave on High (100%) for 4 minutes, until vegetables are tender. Set aside.

2. In a 4-cup measure combine broth mix, noodles, and *1 quart water*; cover with vented plastic wrap and microwave on High (100%) for 4 minutes. Pour noodles and broth into vegetable mixture. Add remaining ingredients; stir until flour is dissolved. Cover with vented plastic wrap and microwave on High (100%) for 6 minutes.

MAKES 4 SERVINGS, ABOUT 1¼ CUPS EACH

Each serving provides: ½ Fat; 1¼ Vegetables; ½ Bread; 15 Optional Calories.

Per serving: 95 calories; 3 g protein; 3 g fat; 15 g carbohydrate; 31 mg calcium; 801 mg sodium; 0 mg cholesterol; 2 g dietary fiber

Reduced cholesterol and fat

Hot Open-Faced Turkey Sandwich with Gravy

PREP TIME: 5 MINUTES
COOKING TIME: 3½ MINUTES
TOTAL TIME: 8½ MINUTES

2 teaspoons reduced-calorie tub margarine
2 slices reduced-calorie rye bread (40 calories per slice)
2 ounces sliced, skinned roast turkey breast
2 tablespoons minced onion
¼ cup lowfat milk (1% milkfat)
2 teaspoons quick-mixing flour
½ packet instant chicken broth and seasoning mix
⅛ teaspoon gravy browning sauce
⅛ teaspoon poultry seasoning
Dash dried thyme and pepper

1. Spread 1 teaspoon margarine on each slice of bread; top each slice with half the turkey. Place open-faced sandwich on a microwavable serving plate.
2. To prepare gravy, place onion in a small microwavable bowl; cover and microwave on High (100%) for 1½ minutes, until onion is softened. Whisk in remaining ingredients and *3 tablespoons water*; microwave on High (100%) for 1 minute, until thickened.
3. Pour gravy over prepared sandwich; microwave at Medium (50%) for 1 minute, until heated through. Serve immediately.

MAKES 1 SERVING

Each serving provides: ¼ Milk; 1 Fat; 2 Proteins; ¼ Vegetable; 1 Bread; 25 Optional Calories.

Per serving: 258 calories; 24 g protein; 7 g fat; 27 g carbohydrate; 135 mg calcium; 833 mg sodium; 42 mg cholesterol; 3 g dietary fiber

Reduced cholesterol and fat

Peanut Butter–Banana Sandwich

PREP TIME: 3 MINUTES
COOKING TIME: 2 MINUTES
TOTAL TIME: 5 MINUTES

1 tablespoon light cream cheese
2 slices reduced-calorie raisin bread (40 calories per slice), toasted
1½ teaspoons raspberry or strawberry all-fruit spread
½ medium banana (3 ounces), sliced
1 tablespoon smooth or chunky peanut butter

1. Spread cream cheese on one slice of toast; top with all-fruit spread and sliced banana.
2. Spread second slice of toast with peanut butter. Close sandwich and cut in half. Serve or place in resealable plastic sandwich bag and refrigerate.

MAKES 1 SERVING

Each serving provides: 1 Fat; 1 Protein; 1 Bread; 1½ Fruits; 33 Optional Calories.

Per serving: 271 calories; 9 g protein; 12 g fat; 37 g carbohydrate; 49 mg calcium; 260 mg sodium; 8 mg cholesterol; 2 g dietary fiber

Reduced cholesterol

Pizza Muffins

PREP TIME: 5 MINUTES
COOKING TIME: 3 MINUTES
TOTAL TIME: 8 MINUTES

2 tablespoons Italian-style tomato sauce	1 ounce Canadian-style bacon, diced
1 English muffin (2 ounces), halved and toasted	1 teaspoon grated Parmesan cheese
1½ ounces part-skim mozzarella cheese, shredded	⅛ teaspoon dried oregano
	⅛ teaspoon dried basil
	5 rinsed drained small black olives, sliced

1. Spoon 1 tablespoon tomato sauce onto each English muffin half. Top each with half the remaining ingredients, in order listed.

2. Broil in toaster oven on top-brown setting until cheese is melted and slightly browned, about 1 minute. Serve immediately.

MAKES 2 SERVINGS

Each serving provides: ¼ Fat; 1½ Proteins; ⅛ Vegetable; 1 Bread; 5 Optional Calories.

Per serving: 159 calories; 11 g protein; 6 g fat; 16 g carbohydrate; 162 mg calcium; 615 mg sodium; 20 mg cholesterol; .4 g dietary fiber

Reduced cholesterol

Macaroni and Cheese

PREP TIME: 5 MINUTES
COOKING TIME: 15 MINUTES
TOTAL TIME: 20 MINUTES

2	teaspoons margarine	¼	teaspoon pepper
1	tablespoon minced shallot	3	ounces Cheddar cheese, grated
2	teaspoons all-purpose flour	3	cups cooked elbow macaroni
1	cup lowfat milk (2% milkfat)	¼	cup pimiento, chopped
2	teaspoons Dijon mustard	¼	teaspoon paprika

1. Preheat oven to 375°F.
2. In a 9-inch skillet heat margarine; add shallot and cook on medium-high heat until softened. Add flour and cook for 1 minute. Add milk, mustard, and pepper and bring to a simmer. Remove from heat and stir in half the cheese until melted.
3. Add macaroni and pimiento; stir until coated with cheese mixture.
4. Spray an 8-inch baking dish with nonstick cooking spray. Add macaroni and cheese mixture; sprinkle evenly with remaining cheese and paprika. Bake for 10 minutes.

MAKES 4 SERVINGS

Each serving provides: ¼ Milk; ½ Fat; 1 Protein; ⅛ Vegetable; 1½ Breads; 13 Optional Calories.

Per serving: 296 calories; 13 g protein; 11 g fat; 36 g carbohydrate; 239 mg calcium; 264 mg sodium; 27 mg cholesterol; 2 g dietary fiber

Eggplant Parmigiana

PREP TIME: 20 MINUTES
COOKING TIME: 56 MINUTES
TOTAL TIME: 1 HOUR, 16 MINUTES

½ cup minced onion
3 garlic cloves, minced
3 cups canned Italian plum tomatoes, seeded and pureed (reserve liquid)
¼ cup plus 2 tablespoons seasoned breadcrumbs
3 tablespoons chopped fresh Italian parsley
¼ teaspoon salt
2 small eggplants, ¾ pound each, sliced ½" thick

1 tablespoon olive oil
1½ cups part-skim ricotta cheese
2¼ ounces shredded part-skim mozzarella cheese
¼ cup thawed frozen egg substitute
2 tablespoons grated Parmesan cheese

1. Spray a 1½-quart saucepan with nonstick cooking spray; add onion and garlic and cook over medium heat until softened. Stir in pureed tomatoes and simmer, uncovered, for 20 minutes, stirring occasionally. Stir in 1 tablespoon breadcrumbs, 1½ tablespoons chopped parsley, and ⅛ teaspoon salt.
2. Preheat broiler and brush both sides of eggplant slices evenly with oil. Broil about 4 inches from heat source for 4 minutes on each side, until golden.
3. Preheat oven to 375°F. In a medium bowl, combine ricotta, 1 ounce mozzarella, egg substitute, remaining parsley and salt, and 1 tablespoon Parmesan cheese.
4. In a 7 × 12-inch baking dish, layer 1 cup tomato sauce, half the eggplant, 2½ tablespoons breadcrumbs, and half the ricotta mixture. Repeat, ending with 1 cup sauce, remaining mozzarella, and Parmesan cheese. Bake for 30 minutes, until sauce bubbles at edges and top layer is melted and golden.

MAKES 4 SERVINGS

Each serving provides: ¾ Fat; 2½ Proteins; 3¾ Vegetables; ½ Bread; 15 Optional Calories.

Per serving: 350 calories; 22 g protein; 15 g fat; 34 g carbohydrate; 525 mg calcium; 991 mg sodium; 40 mg cholesterol; 5 g dietary fiber

Reduced cholesterol

Lasagna

PREP TIME: 15 MINUTES
COOKING TIME: 45 MINUTES
TOTAL TIME: 1 HOUR

1 cup chopped onions	1½ cups part-skim ricotta cheese
3 cups canned Italian plum tomatoes, seeded and pureed (reserve liquid)	¼ cup thawed frozen egg substitute
3 ounces broiled lean ground beef	2 tablespoons grated Parmesan cheese
2 tablespoons chopped fresh Italian parsley	Dash pepper
1 teaspoon dried basil	6 no-boil lasagna noodles (½ ounce each)
¼ teaspoon salt	

1. Spray a 4-quart saucepan with nonstick cooking spray; add onions and cook over medium heat until softened, about 2 minutes. Add pureed tomatoes, ground beef, 1 tablespoon parsley, basil, and ⅛ teaspoon salt. Simmer over low heat, uncovered, until slightly thickened, about 15 minutes.

2. Preheat oven to 375°F.

3. In a medium mixing bowl, stir together remaining ingredients, except for 1 tablespoon Parmesan cheese and the lasagna noodles.

4. Spray an 8-inch square ovenproof baking dish with nonstick cooking spray. Layer 1 cup sauce, 2 lasagna noodles, half the ricotta mixture, 2 lasagna noodles, 1 cup sauce, remaining ricotta mixture, lasagna noodles, sauce, and Parmesan cheese.

5. Bake in preheated oven for 30 minutes, until bubbling at edges. Let stand 10 minutes before cutting.

MAKES 4 SERVINGS

Each serving provides: 2½ Proteins; 2 Vegetables; 1 Bread; 15 Optional Calories.

Per serving: 336 calories; 23 g protein; 13 g fat; 31 g carbohydrate; 361 mg calcium; 629 mg sodium; 49 mg cholesterol; 2 g dietary fiber

Reduced cholesterol

Spicy Hamburger Pie

PREP TIME: 10 MINUTES
COOKING TIME: 12 MINUTES
TOTAL TIME: 22 MINUTES

12 saltine crackers (1½ ounces), finely crushed	½ cup prepared medium-thick chunky salsa
1 tablespoon plus 1 teaspoon reduced-calorie tub margarine	½ cup reduced-sodium tomato sauce
½ cup minced onion	1 teaspoon chili seasoning
5 ounces lean ground beef	¾ ounce reduced-fat Cheddar cheese, shredded
½ cup chopped red or green bell pepper	2 tablespoons light sour cream (optional)

1. In a small bowl, combine saltines, margarine, and 2 tablespoons minced onion. Spray a 7½-inch microwavable pie plate with nonstick cooking spray. Press mixture on bottom and up sides of the plate to form a crust. Microwave on High (100%) for 2 minutes, rotating plate a quarter turn after 1 minute. Set aside.

2. Crumble meat on a microwavable roasting rack; cover and microwave on High (100%) for 1½ minutes, until meat loses its pink color. Stir meat halfway through cooking time. Set aside.

3. Spray a 1-quart microwavable casserole with nonstick cooking spray. Add remaining onion, chopped pepper, and *1 tablespoon water*; cover and microwave on High (100%) for 2 minutes, stirring after 1 minute. Stir in cooked beef, salsa, tomato sauce, and chili seasoning; microwave on Medium/High (70%) for 5 minutes, stirring halfway through cooking time.

4. Transfer meat mixture to prepared crust; top with shredded cheese. Microwave on Medium (50%) for 1 minute, until cheese is melted. Top with sour cream, if using. Serve immediately.

MAKES 2 SERVINGS

Each serving provides: 1 Fat; 2½ Proteins; 2 Vegetables; 1 Bread.

Per serving: 379 calories; 16 g protein; 23 g fat; 28 g carbohydrate; 22 mg calcium; 826 mg sodium; 53 mg cholesterol; 2 g dietary fiber

Fish Cakes

PREP TIME: 10 MINUTES
COOKING TIME: 40 MINUTES
TOTAL TIME: 50 MINUTES

1 pound, 2 ounces scrod fillet, coarsely chopped in food processor
3 tablespoons seasoned breadcrumbs
6 saltine crackers, crushed
1 tablespoon plus 1 teaspoon vegetable oil
¾ cup diced mushrooms
¼ cup diced onion
¼ cup diced red bell pepper
¼ cup diced green bell pepper
3 tablespoons all-purpose flour
½ cup clam juice
1 tablespoon chopped fresh Italian parsley
Dash salt and pepper
1 egg, lightly beaten

1. In a medium mixing bowl, combine scrod, breadcrumbs, and crushed saltines.

2. In a 9-inch nonstick skillet heat 1 teaspoon oil; add diced vegetables and cook over medium heat for 3 minutes, until softened. Add flour and stir until well combined; stir in clam juice, parsley, salt, and pepper. Simmer over low heat for 1 minute.

3. Add vegetable mixture to scrod; stir in egg until well combined. Form mixture into 12 equal-sized patties.

4. In 9-inch nonstick skillet heat 1 teaspoon oil; add 4 patties and cook over medium heat for 6 minutes on each side, until cooked through. Transfer cooked fish cakes to serving platter; keep warm. Repeat twice, using all remaining ingredients. Serve warm fish cakes immediately.

MAKES 4 SERVINGS, 3 FISH CAKES EACH

Each serving provides: 1 Fat; 2 Proteins; ¾ Vegetable; ¾ Bread; 5 Optional Calories.

Per serving: 239 calories; 27 g protein; 7 g fat; 14 g carbohydrate; 39 mg calcium; 435 mg sodium; 111 mg cholesterol; 1 g dietary fiber

Reduced fat

Fisherman's Pie

PREP TIME: 10 MINUTES
COOKING TIME: 15 MINUTES
TOTAL TIME: 25 MINUTES

2	teaspoons margarine	⅛	teaspoon salt
¼	cup finely chopped onion	⅛	teaspoon pepper
2	teaspoons all-purpose flour		Dash nutmeg
1	ounce drained canned chopped clams (packed in water); reserve ¼ cup liquid	3	ounces scrod or sole fillet
		2	ounces sea scallops, cut into ½-inch pieces
1	cup lowfat milk (2% milkfat)	1½	ounces uncooked potato flakes (about ¾ cup)

1. Preheat broiler. Spray a ½-quart ovenproof casserole with nonstick cooking spray.
2. In a 1-quart saucepan melt 1 teaspoon margarine; add onion and cook over medium heat until softened, about 2 minutes. Sprinkle flour over onions; cook, stirring frequently, for 1 minute. Stir in reserved clam liquid, 2 tablespoons milk, the salt, pepper, and nutmeg. Cook over medium-high heat, stirring constantly, until sauce thickens, about 2 minutes.
3. Stir in scrod, scallops, and chopped clams; cook over medium heat until scrod flakes easily when tested with a fork, about 3 minutes. Transfer to prepared casserole; keep warm.
4. In a ½-quart saucepan heat remaining milk, margarine, and *2 tablespoons water* over high heat until boiling; remove from heat. Using a fork, stir in potato flakes until mixture has a soft consistency. Spoon mashed potatoes evenly over fish, sealing all edges. Place under broiler until golden brown. Serve immediately.

MAKES 2 SERVINGS

Each serving provides: ½ Milk; 1 Fat; 1½ Proteins; ¼ Vegetable; 1 Bread; 25 Optional Calories.

Per serving: 272 calories; 22 g protein; 7 g fat; 29 g carbohydrate; 251 mg calcium; 357 mg sodium; 47 mg cholesterol; .4 g dietary fiber

Reduced fat

Lemon Chicken

PREP TIME: 10 MINUTES
COOKING TIME: 20 MINUTES
MARINATING TIME: 20 MINUTES
TOTAL TIME: 50 MINUTES

Marinade

3 tablespoons lemon juice	2 teaspoons olive or vegetable oil
1 teaspoon chopped fresh oregano	1 teaspoon cornstarch dissolved in ¼ cup chicken broth
1 teaspoon minced shallot	1 tablespoon capers, rinsed and drained
½ teaspoon dry mustard	
Dash salt and pepper	

12 ounces chicken legs and thighs, skin removed

1. In a stainless-steel or glass bowl combine marinade ingredients. Add chicken and toss to coat. Cover and refrigerate 20 minutes.

2. In a 9-inch skillet, heat oil. Drain chicken; reserve marinade. Cook chicken, covered, over medium heat for 15 minutes on each side. Remove chicken to serving platter and keep warm.

3. In same skillet heat reserved marinade to boiling; gradually add dissolved cornstarch; stir until sauce boils and thickens, about 1 minute. Add capers and stir until thoroughly heated. Pour sauce over chicken and serve immediately.

MAKES 2 SERVINGS

Each serving provides: 1 Fat; 3 Proteins; 10 Optional Calories.

Per serving: 220 calories; 24 g protein; 12 g fat; 3 g carbohydrate; 19 mg calcium; 382 mg sodium; 80 mg cholesterol; 0 g dietary fiber

Reduced sodium

Savory Chicken Loaf

PREP TIME: 5 MINUTES
COOKING TIME: 50 MINUTES
TOTAL TIME: 55 MINUTES

½ cup chopped onion
2 garlic cloves, minced
½ cup thawed and well-drained frozen chopped spinach
1 ounce reduced-sodium boiled ham, minced
12 ounces ground chicken
⅓ cup lowfat cottage cheese (1% milkfat)
¼ cup thawed frozen egg substitute

¼ cup plus 2 tablespoons seasoned breadcrumbs
2 tablespoons fresh chopped basil or Italian parsley
2 tablespoons grated Parmesan cheese, divided
Dash salt, pepper, and nutmeg

1. Preheat oven to 375°F.
2. Spray a 9-inch nonstick skillet with nonstick cooking spray; add onion and garlic and cook over medium heat until softened, about 2 minutes. Stir in spinach and ham and cook for 2 more minutes, stirring occasionally; set aside to cool.
3. In a medium mixing bowl combine spinach mixture and remaining ingredients, except for 1 tablespoon Parmesan cheese.
4. Spray a 7 × 11-inch glass baking dish with nonstick cooking spray. Shape meat mixture into a 3½ × 7-inch loaf; transfer to prepared baking dish. Sprinkle loaf with remaining Parmesan cheese and bake in preheated oven for 45 minutes. Let stand for 5 minutes; cut into 8 equal slices.

MAKES 4 SERVINGS, 2 SLICES EACH

Each serving provides: 3 Proteins; ½ Vegetable; ½ Bread; 15 Optional Calories.

Per serving: 230 calories; 23 g protein; 10 g fat; 12 g carbohydrate; 134 mg calcium; 622 mg sodium; 77 mg cholesterol; 1 g dietary fiber

Veal Stew with Dumplings

PREP TIME: 15 MINUTES
COOKING TIME: 1 HOUR, 20 MINUTES
TOTAL TIME: 1 HOUR, 35 MINUTES

13 ounces boneless cubed veal (shoulder cut for stewing)
1 cup plus 2 tablespoons buttermilk baking mix
1 tablespoon plus 1 teaspoon vegetable oil
1 cup diced carrots
1 cup quartered small mushrooms
1 cup frozen pearl onions
1 cup skim milk
½ cup dry white wine
1 packet instant chicken broth and seasoning mix
1 teaspoon chopped fresh thyme or ¼ teaspoon dried thyme
1 bay leaf
1 tablespoon chopped fresh parsley
Dash salt and pepper

1. In a small mixing bowl dredge veal in 2 tablespoons buttermilk baking mix until meat is coated on all sides.

2. In a 3-quart saucepan heat oil; add veal and cook over medium-high heat, stirring frequently, until lightly golden, about 3 minutes. Add carrots, mushrooms, and onions; cook, stirring frequently, for 1 minute.

3. Add ⅔ cup milk, the wine, broth mix, thyme, bay leaf, and ⅓ cup water. Stir, scraping bottom of pan to loosen any particles. Reduce heat and simmer, partly covered, stirring occasionally, for 55 minutes. Stir in parsley, salt, and pepper.

4. To prepare dumplings, in a small mixing bowl stir together remaining buttermilk baking mix and ⅓ cup milk. Drop batter by rounded tablespoonfuls onto the stew to make 8 dumplings. Cook over medium heat, uncovered, for 10 minutes. Cook, covered, for 10 more minutes over low heat. Serve immediately.

MAKES 4 SERVINGS

Each serving provides: ¼ Milk; 1 Fat; 2½ Proteins; 1½ Vegetables; 1½ Breads; 58 Optional Calories.

Per serving: 350 calories; 24 g protein; 11 g fat; 32 g carbohydate; 174 mg calcium; 807 mg sodium; 80 mg cholesterol; 2 g dietary fiber

Reduced fat

Kasha Stuffed Peppers

PREP TIME: 10 MINUTES
COOKING TIME: 50 MINUTES
TOTAL TIME: 60 MINUTES

4 ounces (about ⅔ cup) buckwheat groats (kasha)	1 tablespoon tahini (sesame paste)
¼ cup egg substitute	1 packet instant vegetable or onion mix
1 tablespoon vegetable oil	½ teaspoon dried Italian seasoning
½ cup chopped onion	Dash salt and pepper
4 garlic cloves, minced	4 medium red or green bell peppers
½ cup diced celery	
½ cup diced carrot	

1. Heat a 9-inch skillet sprayed with nonstick cooking spray; add kasha and egg substitute and cook, stirring, for 3 minutes, until grains are separated and dry.

2. In a 3-quart saucepan heat oil; add onion and garlic and cook for 1 minute. Add celery and carrot and cook for 2 more minutes, until celery is tender. Add prepared kasha, remaining ingredients except peppers, and *1⅓ cups water*. Bring mixture to a boil; reduce heat and simmer, covered, for 15 minutes. Remove from heat and let stand, covered, for 10 minutes.

3. Preheat oven to 375°F. Fill a bowl with ice water. Slice tops off peppers and reserve. Remove seeds and membranes, being careful not to break the shells. Place shells in a 6-quart saucepan filled with boiling water. Parboil peppers for 3 minutes, then plunge into ice water. Drain on paper towels.

4. Fill shells evenly with the kasha mixture; cover with pepper tops. Place peppers and *¼ cup water* in a 1-quart ovenproof casserole; bake for 20 minutes or until peppers test fork-tender.

MAKES 4 SERVINGS, 1 PEPPER EACH

Each serving provides: 1 Fat; ½ Protein; 2¾ Vegetables; 1 Bread; 3 Optional Calories.

Per serving: 221 calories; 8 g protein; 7 g fat; 35 g carbohydrate; 61 mg calcium; 305 mg sodium; 0 mg cholesterol; 6 g dietary fiber

Reduced cholesterol and fat

Glazed Butternut Squash

PREP TIME: 5 MINUTES
COOKING TIME: 9 MINUTES
TOTAL TIME: 14 MINUTES

2	cups pared cubed butternut squash, ¾" cubes	1	tablespoon reduced-calorie pancake syrup (25 calories per tablespoon)
1	cup frozen pearl onions		
1	ounce chopped walnuts	1	tablespoon apple juice
1	tablespoon plus 1 teaspoon reduced-calorie tub margarine, melted	½	teaspoon cornstarch
		½	teaspoon lemon juice
		½	teaspoon cider vinegar
			Dash salt and pepper

1. Place squash and *1 tablespoon water* in a 3-quart microwavable casserole; cover and microwave on High (100%) for 3 minutes, stirring to rearrange squash halfway through cooking time.

2. Add onions; cover and microwave on High (100%) for 1 more minute, until squash is fork-tender. Drain squash and onions.

3. Place walnuts on a microwavable plate; microwave on High (100%) for 2 minutes.

4. Whisk remaining ingredients together in a small microwavable mixing bowl; cover and microwave on High (100%) for 1 minute, until glaze has thickened. Pour glaze over squash and onions; add nuts and toss until glaze is evenly distributed. Microwave, covered, at Medium/High (70%) power for 2 minutes, until heated through.

MAKES 4 SERVINGS

Each serving provides: 1 Fat; ¼ Protein; ½ Vegetable; ½ Bread; 10 Optional Calories.

Per serving: 120 calories; 2 g protein; 6 g fat; 16 g carbohydrate; 58 mg calcium; 87 mg sodium; 0 mg cholesterol; .4 g dietary fiber

Reduced cholesterol and sodium

Barbecued Corn on the Cob

PREP TIME: 5 MINUTES
COOKING TIME: 10 MINUTES
TOTAL TIME: 15 MINUTES

¼ cup mild salsa
1 teaspoon chopped fresh Italian parsley
2 small ears corn on the cob (5″ long)

⅛ teaspoon salt
⅛ teaspoon pepper

1. In a small mixing bowl, combine salsa and parsley. Preheat barbecue grill. (Use high setting if cooking with gas grill.)
2. Cut two 12 × 19-inch pieces of aluminum foil. Place corn in center of each piece of foil; sprinkle with salt and pepper.
3. Spoon half the salsa mixture over each ear of corn; turn corn to coat. Fold foil to enclose corn.
4. Place foil packets on preheated grill; cook for 10 minutes, turning every 2 to 3 minutes. Carefully open foil packets and transfer corn to serving dish; serve immediately.

MAKES 2 SERVINGS

Each serving provides: ¼ Vegetable; 1 Bread.

Per serving: 75 calories; 2 g protein; 1 g fat; 17 g carbohydrate; 4 mg calcium; 330 mg sodium; 0 mg cholesterol; 3 g dietary fiber

Reduced cholesterol and fat

Vegetables Au Gratin

PREP TIME: 5 MINUTES
COOKING TIME: 7 MINUTES
TOTAL TIME: 12 MINUTES

½ cup sliced yellow squash
½ small eggplant, sliced
  ¼" thick
¼ cup sliced onion
¼ cup diced red bell
  pepper
Dash salt and pepper

3 tablespoons dried
  breadcrumbs
¾ ounce shredded
  Cheddar cheese
1 teaspoon chopped fresh
  basil

1. In a 6-inch round microwavable shallow casserole, layer squash and eggplant. Cover evenly with onion and bell pepper; sprinkle with salt and pepper. Cover with vented plastic wrap and microwave on High (100%) for 6 minutes, until vegetables are tender-crisp.
2. In a small bowl combine breadcrumbs, cheese, and basil. Sprinkle evenly over vegetables. Cover with vented plastic wrap and microwave on High (100%) for 1 minute, until cheese melts.

MAKES 2 SERVINGS

Each serving provides: ½ Protein; 1½ Vegetables; ½ Bread.

Per serving: 118 calories; 5 g protein; 4 g fat; 16 g carbohydrate; 136 mg calcium; 206 mg sodium; 12 mg cholesterol; 3 g dietary fiber

Reduced cholesterol

Cole Slaw

PREP TIME: 12 MINUTES
TOTAL TIME: 12 MINUTES

1½ cups shredded red
cabbage
1½ cups shredded green
cabbage
½ cup grated carrot
¼ cup sliced scallions
¼ cup diced yellow bell
pepper
¾ cup plain lowfat yogurt

¼ cup crushed pineapple,
no sugar added
1 tablespoon chopped
fresh Italian parsley
1 teaspoon prepared Dijon
mustard
¼ teaspoon garlic powder
Dash salt and pepper

1. In a medium mixing bowl, combine vegetables.
2. In a small mixing bowl, combine all remaining ingredients.
3. Pour yogurt mixture over vegetables and toss to coat. Cover and refrigerate until ready to serve.

MAKES 4 SERVINGS

Each serving provides: ¼ Milk; 2 Vegetables; 10 Optional Calories.

Per serving: 61 calories; 3 g protein; 1 g fat; 11 g carbohydrate; 115 mg calcium; 114 mg sodium; 3 mg cholesterol; 2 g dietary fiber

Reduced cholesterol, fat, and sodium

Individual Cherry Cobblers

PREP TIME: 5 MINUTES
COOKING TIME: 25 MINUTES
TOTAL TIME: 30 MINUTES

24	large sweet cherries, pitted (6 ounces)	1	teaspoon lemon juice
1	tablespoon plus 2 teaspoons granulated sugar	½	teaspoon lemon zest
		3	tablespoons all-purpose flour
2	teaspoons cornstarch	2	teaspoons margarine, melted
1	teaspoon vanilla extract	½	teaspoon cinnamon

1. Preheat oven to 350°F.
2. Divide cherries evenly between two 6-ounce custard cups. In a small bowl, combine 2 teaspoons sugar, the cornstarch, vanilla, lemon juice, and zest; add half the mixture to each cup and mix to combine with cherries.
3. In the same small bowl, combine the flour, remaining 1 tablespoon sugar, margarine, and cinnamon until mixture has a crumb-like consistency. Sprinkle evenly over cherry mixtures.
4. Bake for 20 minutes; turn oven to 375°F and bake for 5 additional minutes.

MAKES 2 SERVINGS

Each serving provides: 1 Fat; ½ Bread; 1 Fruit; 60 Optional Calories.

Per serving: 192 calories; 2 g protein; 5 g fat; 36 g carbohydrate; 23 mg calcium; 46 mg sodium; 0 mg cholesterol; 2 g dietary fiber

Reduced cholesterol, fat, and sodium

Meringue-Capped Rice Pudding

PREP TIME: 10 MINUTES
COOKING TIME: 40 MINUTES
TOTAL TIME: 50 MINUTES

1 cup lowfat milk
(1% milkfat)
½ cup evaporated
skimmed milk
2 tablespoons dark raisins
1 tablespoon plus
1 teaspoon
granulated sugar

Dash salt
2 ounces uncooked
medium-grain rice
(about ⅓ cup)
1 teaspoon vanilla extract
½ teaspoon grated lemon
zest
1 egg white

1. In a 1½-quart saucepan combine milk, raisins, 1 tablespoon sugar, and salt. Bring to a boil over medium-high heat; stir in rice. Reduce heat to low and cook, covered, for 20 minutes, stirring every 3 to 4 minutes.

2. Stir in *3 tablespoons water* and cook, covered, for an additional 5 minutes. Stir in vanilla and lemon zest. Preheat oven to 350°F.

3. To prepare meringue, in a small bowl, using an electric mixer on high speed, beat egg white until foamy. Gradually add remaining 1 teaspoon sugar and continue to beat on high speed until egg white is stiff but not dry.

4. Spray two 10-ounce custard cups with nonstick cooking spray; spoon half the cooked pudding into each cup. Spread ½ meringue over each pudding, sealing all edges. Bake in preheated oven for 10 minutes, until meringue is golden brown. Let cool for 20 minutes; serve chilled.

MAKES 2 SERVINGS

Each serving provides: 1 Milk; 1 Bread; ½ Fruit; 50 Optional Calories.

Per serving: 297 calories; 13 g protein; 4 g fat; 52 g carbohydrate; 348 mg calcium; 230 mg sodium; 12 mg cholesterol; 1 g dietary fiber

Reduced cholesterol and fat

Microwave Fruit Compote

PREP TIME: 7 MINUTES
COOKING TIME: 3 MINUTES
TOTAL TIME: 10 MINUTES

1	small pear, pared, cored, and sliced	½	teaspoon granulated sugar
3	medium prunes, pitted and halved		One 3-inch cinnamon stick
1	ounce (2 tablespoons) Port wine	¼	teaspoon grated orange zest
½	cup canned mandarin orange sections with 2 tablespoons juice (no sugar added)		Whipped topping (optional)

1. In a 1-quart microwavable casserole combine pear slices, prunes, wine, juice from orange sections, sugar, cinnamon stick, and *1 tablespoon water*. Cover and microwave on High (100%) for 2 minutes, until liquid boils and pear tests fork-tender.
2. Stir in orange sections and orange zest. Microwave, covered, on Low (30%) for 1 minute, until orange sections are just warmed through. Remove and discard cinnamon stick.
3. Divide compote between two 8-ounce serving dishes; add topping if using.

MAKES 2 SERVINGS

Each serving provides: 1½ Fruits; 30 Optional Calories.

Per serving: 125 calories; 1 g protein; .4 g fat; 28 g carbohydrate; 36 mg calcium; 5 mg sodium; 0 mg cholesterol; 3 g dietary fiber

Reduced cholesterol, fat, and sodium

Spice Muffins with Maple Icing

PREP TIME: 5 MINUTES
COOKING TIME: 25 MINUTES
TOTAL TIME: 30 MINUTES

1 cup plus 2 tablespoons all-purpose flour	½ cup lowfat milk (2% milkfat)
2 tablespoons firmly packed light-brown sugar	1 egg
	2 tablespoons vegetable oil
1 teaspoon baking powder	2 tablespoons confectioners' sugar
1 teaspoon cinnamon	¼ teaspoon maple flavoring
½ teaspoon nutmeg	
¼ teaspoon allspice	
¼ teaspoon cloves	

1. Preheat oven to 400°F.
2. In a medium mixing bowl combine flour, sugar, baking powder, and spices; set aside.
3. In a 2-cup liquid measure whisk together milk, egg, and oil until well combined; add to flour mixture and stir until batter is just moistened (do no beat or overmix).
4. Spray six 2½-inch diameter muffin pan cups with nonstick cooking spray and fill each with an equal amount of batter (each will be about ¾ full). Bake in preheated oven for 25 minutes (until muffins are brown and a toothpick inserted in center comes out clean). Invert muffins onto wire rack.
5. To prepare icing, in a small bowl whisk together sugar, *1 teaspoon water*, and maple flavoring. With a pastry brush, brush tops of muffins evenly with icing.

MAKES 6 SERVINGS, 1 MUFFIN EACH

Each serving provides: 1 Fat; 1 Bread; 62 Optional Calories.

Per serving: 178 calories; 4 g protein; 6 g fat; 27 g carbohydrate; 78 mg calcium; 94 mg sodium; 37 mg cholesterol; 1 g dietary fiber

Reduced sodium

Strawberry Meringue Tarts with Chocolate Syrup

PREP TIME: 10 MINUTES
COOKING TIME: 40 MINUTES
TOTAL TIME: 50 MINUTES

1 egg white	1 cup strawberries, sliced
¼ teaspoon cream of tartar	1 tablespoon whipped topping
1 tablespoon granulated sugar	2 teaspoons chocolate syrup
½ teaspoon unsweetened cocoa powder	

1. Line a baking sheet with parchment paper; set aside. In a medium mixing bowl, using an electric mixer at medium speed, beat egg white until foamy; add cream of tartar, sugar, and cocoa and continue beating until stiff peaks form.

2. Preheat oven to 275°F.

3. Using a pastry bag fitted with star tip, fill bag with egg white mixture and pipe some of mixture onto lined baking sheet, forming outlines of two 3½ × 3-inch hearts (if pastry bag is not available, spoon mixture onto baking sheet); fill center of each heart with an equal amount of remaining meringue mixture.

4. Bake until golden and crisp, 40 minutes. Turn off oven; let meringue stand in oven for 20 minutes longer to dry. Carefully remove meringues from paper to wire rack and let cool.

5. To serve, arrange strawberries decoratively over each meringue and place whipped topping in center of heart; drizzle with chocolate syrup; serve immediately.

MAKES 2 SERVINGS

Each serving provides: ½ Fruit; 68 Optional Calories.

Per serving: 75 calories; 2 g protein; 1 g fat; 16 g carbohydrate; 15 mg calcium; 36 mg sodium; .3 mg cholesterol; 2 g dietary fiber

Reduced cholesterol, fat, and sodium

Apple Crumb Pie

PREP TIME: 15 MINUTES
COOKING TIME: 40 MINUTES
TOTAL TIME: 55 MINUTES

½ refrigerated ready-to-bake 9-inch pie crust
6 tablespoons all-purpose flour
3 small Golden Delicious apples (4 ounces each), pared, cored, and sliced
2 tablespoons dried currants or dark raisins
1 tablespoon granulated sugar

¾ teaspoon cinnamon
⅛ teaspoon nutmeg
½ teaspoon grated lemon zest
2 tablespoons plus 2 teaspoons reduced-calorie tub margarine

1. Preheat oven to 425°F. Shape pastry into a ball; sprinkle ½ teaspoon of the flour onto a work surface and roll pastry into an 8½-inch circle. Place pastry in a 7½-inch pie plate sprayed with nonstick cooking spray. Prick pastry with fork. Line pastry with aluminum foil and fill with dried beans. Prebake crust for 10 minutes; cool on a rack for 10 minutes. Remove beans and foil. Reduce oven heat to 350°F.

2. In a medium bowl, combine apples, currants, 1 teaspoon sugar, ½ teaspoon cinnamon, and the nutmeg; arrange fruit mixture in crust.

3. In a small bowl, stir together remaining flour, sugar, cinnamon, and lemon zest. Using a pastry blender, cut in margarine until mixture resembles coarse crumbs. Sprinkle crumb mixture evenly over fruit. Bake for 20 minutes at 350°F; bake for another 10 minutes at 375°F, until topping is golden.

MAKES 4 SERVINGS

Each serving provides: 1 Fat; 1½ Breads; 1 Fruit; 65 Optional Calories.

Per serving: 264 calories; 2 g protein; 12 g fat; 38 g carbohydrate; 16 mg calcium; 179 mg sodium; 8 mg cholesterol; 2 g dietary fiber

Reduced cholesterol and sodium

Weight Watchers Metric Conversion Table

WEIGHT

To Change	To	Multiply by
Ounces	Grams	30.0
Pounds	Kilograms	0.48

VOLUME

To Change	To	Multiply by
Teaspoons	Milliliters	5.0
Tablespoons	Milliliters	15.0
Cups	Milliliters	250.0
Cups	Liters	0.25
Pints	Liters	0.5
Quarts	Liters	1.0
Gallons	Liters	4.0

LENGTH

To Change	To	Multiply by
Inches	Millimeters	25.0
Inches	Centimeters	2.5
Feet	Centimeters	30.0
Yards	Meters	0.9

TEMPERATURE

To change degrees Fahrenheit to degrees Celsius subtract 32° and multiply by $\frac{5}{9}$.

Oven Temperatures

Degrees Fahrenheit	= Degrees Celsius	Degrees Fahrenheit	= Degrees Celsius
250	120	400	200
275	140	425	220
300	150	450	230
325	160	475	250
350	180	500	260
375	190	525	270

METRIC SYMBOLS

Symbol	= Metric Unit	Symbol	= Metric Unit
g	gram	°C	degrees Celsius
kg	kilogram	mm	millimeter
ml	milliliter	cm	centimeter
l = liter		m	meter

Dry and Liquid Measure Equivalents

Teaspoons	Tablespoons	Cups	Fluid Ounces
3 teaspoons	1 tablespoon		½ fluid ounce
6 teaspoons	2 tablespoons	⅛ cup	1 fluid ounce
12 teaspoons	4 tablespoons	¼ cup	2 fluid ounces
16 teaspoons	5 tablespoons plus 1 teaspoon	⅓ cup	
18 teaspoons	6 tablespoons	⅓ cup plus 2 teaspoons	3 fluid ounces
24 teaspoons	8 tablespoons	½ cup	4 fluid ounces
30 teaspoons	10 tablespoons	½ cup plus 2 tablespoons	5 fluid ounces
32 teaspoons	10 tablespoons plus 2 teaspoons	⅔ cup	
36 teaspoons	12 tablespoons	¾ cup	6 fluid ounces
42 teaspoons	14 tablespoons	1 cup less 2 tablespoons	7 fluid ounces
48 teaspoons	16 tablespoons	1 cup	8 fluid ounces
96 teaspoons	32 tablespoons	2 cups (1 pint)	16 fluid ounces
		4 cups (1 quart)	32 fluid ounces

Note: Measurements of less than ⅛ teaspoon are considered a dash or a pinch.